MW00438628

Introducing
Educational
Reconstruction:

The Philosophy
and Practice
of Transforming
Society
through Education

By The Society
for Educational Reconstruction

Contributing Authors:
Darrol Bussler, Frances L. O'Neil, Angela Raffel,
Frank Andrews Stone, and T. Mathai Thomas,

Edited by Susan Roberts and Darrol Bussler

Introducing Educational Reconstruction:
The Philosophy and Practice
of Transforming Society through Education

By The Society for Educational Reconstruction

Contributing Authors:
Darrol Bussler, Frances L. O'Neil, Angela Raffel,
Frank Andrews Stone, and T. Mathai Thomas,

Edited by Susan Roberts and Darrol Bussler

Published by:
Caddo Gap Press
3145 Geary Boulevard, Suite 275
San Francisco, California 94118, U.S.A.
Alan H. Jones, Publisher

Copyright 1997 by The Society for Educational Reconstruction

ISBN 1-880192-22-5

Price $14.95

Library of Congress Cataloging-in-Publication Data

Introducing educational reconstruction : the philosophy and practice
  of transforming society through education / by the Society for
  Educational Reconstruction ; contributing authors, Angela Raffel ...
  [et al.] ; edited by Susan Roberts.
      p.   cm.
  Includes bibliographical references.
  ISBN 1-880192-22-5 (alk. paper)
  1. Education--Social aspects. 2. Social change--Study and
teaching.   I. Raffel, Angela.   II. Roberts, Susan, 1950-
III. Society for Educational Reconstruction.
LC191.4.I58   1997
370.11'5--dc21   97-3138
                                                         CIP

2

CONTENTS

Dedication 4

Preface
Introducing Educational Reconstruction 5

Introduction
In Praise of Educational Reconstruction 7
    By Angela Raffel

Chapter One
Agents of Socio-Educational Change:
Educational Reconstruction's Origins 15
    By Frank Andrews Stone

Chapter Two
Social Problems and Issues:
Views of an Educational Reconstructionist 33
    By T. Mathai Thomas

Chapter Three
Some Basic Tenets
of Educational Reconstruction 49
    By Darrol Bussler

Chapter Four
Educational Reconstruction
in the Future 121
    By Frances L. O'Neil

Contributing Authors 133

About The Society for Educational Reconstruction 135

DEDICATION

Introducing Educational Reconstruction is a gesture of thanksgiving for the life and professional career of Dr. Jay M. Smith. Jay was born in New London, Connecticut, on February 24, 1943. He taught in the Baltimore and Pittsburgh public schools and as a professor of educational psychology at Indiana University of Pennsylvania, Hofstra University, and Adelphi University. His teaching and writing were distinguished by his commitments to humanistic psychology, gender studies, and social justice. Jay was a chairperson of The Society for Educational Reconstruction (SER) and active in many SER endeavors, including the introduction of the annual Theodore Brameld Lecture beginning in the late 1970s. Tragically, Jay died suddenly in mid-career on June 22, 1985, due to a biking accident at Rockville Center, New York. The SER Executive Committee has dedicated this publication to the memory of Jay M. Smith.

Preface

INTRODUCING EDUCATIONAL RECONSTRUCTION

As the authors presented in this volume articulately and amply illustrate, the philosophy of Educational Reconstruction has strong roots in twentieth century America and significant promise for the twenty-first century and beyond. Yet when educational philosophy is taught in schools and colleges of education, discussed in the corridors and teachers' lounges of schools across the country and around the world, and analyzed at professional conferences and educational conventions, typically Educational Reconstruction receives little or only marginal if any attention.

What accounts for this neglect? While Theodore Brameld is regularly, and rightly, celebrated as one of the great educational philosophers of this century, why is the philosophy of Educational Reconstruction to which he contributed so much consistently ignored? Is it, perhaps, that as the merits of pragmatism and Progressive Education have been demeaned and belittled over recent decades and characterized as too radical, then the even more radical and challenging views of Educational Reconstruction have been set aside by the educational and political mainstream, in hopes that all that is not conservative will be forgotten?

It is the mission of the Society for Educational Reconstruction (SER) to assure that no such forgetting takes place. The purpose of this volume, *Introducing Educational Reconstruction*, is to provide an historical, contemporary, and future-oriented discussion of the philosophy of Educational Reconstruction, in a form suitable for the professional reading of any and all educators, for use in introductory and advanced studies in teacher education and related fields, and for consideration by policymakers and other concerned citizens.

The five participating authors are respected educational scholars and practitioners as well as active and committed leaders of SER. They discuss Educational Reconstruction from both personal and professional experience, providing a strong philosophical context as well as practical examples appropriate to this action-oriented educational philosophy.

As a long-time member of SER it is my great pleasure to serve as publisher for this volume. It bears a significant message for the educational community and the broader world society. May it be read and understood with the same passion as it has been written and published.

—Alan H. Jones
Member, Executive Committee,
The Society for Educational Reconstruction,
and Publisher, Caddo Gap Press

Introduction

In Praise
of Educational
Reconstruction

By Angela Raffel

Historical Roots

> Educational Reconstruction is a philosophy based on examining
> cultural premises and implementing conflict and social change
> theory. It has been advocated by notable educators, among them
> Theodore Brameld, who sought desirable social development and
> progress through exploring alternatives for the future with teenag-
> ers and their teachers.

This defining statement by Frank Andrews Stone is an excellent
introduction to the origins of Educational Reconstruction. Born out
of the struggle for human rights and social justice, Educational
Reconstruction has ineluctably emerged in the minds of many scholars and practitioners who, in concert, have concluded that education
can and should be a tool for social transformation and that the great
problems faced by humanity should be the basis of the school
curriculum. Examples of pioneers testing out such theories in action
are numerous.

Myles Horton is credited with developing the Highlander Research and Education Center at New Market, Tennessee. He worked

with African Americans on Johns Island to achieve access to literacy for them. Through education, they learned how to participate in democratic processes; they became empowered and self-directed.

Morris R. Mitchell, through his concept of community education, was able to develop a broad perspective on world education, envisioning global peace and order. Having tested out the theory of Educational Reconstruction, he asserted that the philosophy—one of future orientation—addressed itself to facing and accepting the pressing human problems in an ever-changing society.

William O. Stanley claimed that, to study the salient conflicts and confusions of our time, there must be cooperative inquiry leading toward consensus about action to be taken concerning nuclear threats, environmental fears, multicultural needs, and feminist demands.

Educational Reconstruction has been widely implemented internationally. Mohandas Karamchard Gandhi carried out reconstruction in South Africa and India. Ismail Hakki Tonguch formed the Turkish Village Institute Movement. Paulo Freire discussed with people their struggles against injustices and their fight for human freedom from pain, oppression, and abandonment. Lasting social changes can come about only through long-term educational processes. All of these pioneers put into practice their belief in reconstructional thought and action.

John Dewey also provided a perspective on Educational Reconstruction in his "reconstruction of human experiences." Some of his recommendations for education are stated clearly in terms of that philosophy.

W.E.B. DuBois applied this methodology in his early studies of problems of Blacks. The fight of African Americans against oppression was advanced through his application of Educational Reconstruction principles.

This philosophy is also embodied in the work of George Counts who clearly states his position in his famous pamphlet, *Dare the School Build a New Social Order?* which appeared in 1932. This position was also confirmed by other educators, among them, Harold Rugg.

It is this history that Stone describes in the first chapter of this volume. As he indicates, Educational Reconstruction continues today. As a philosophy it provides a sound approach to education, for it stems from an understanding and acknowledgement of the human condition, ever seeking social improvement.

Implementation of the Philosophy

In the second chapter, T. Mathai Thomas discusses a significant means for the implementation of Educational Reconstruction: through students in his education courses. In questioning them about social conditions, having them isolate and define major problems in America—such as violence, corruption, environmental issues, unemployment, drug abuse, and financial insecurity—he motivates them to thought and action beyond the classroom. Students' recognition of these issues promotes on-going change and radical reform by creating an orientation to an improved world.

Reconstructionists insist upon transformation of the culture through a willingness to experiment with hands-on experience. Creative ideas call for action and practice. Through the Putney Graduate School in Vermont, founded by Mitchell, Thomas conducted an experiment to explore "the culture of poverty." In his "ninety-nine days on ninety-nine dollars" experiment, he confirmed Mitchell's teaching that the key word is action in relation to community.

Theodore Brameld, then teaching at Boston University, introduced Thomas to the need for a culturalogical approach to a modern world always in paradoxical "crisis," a world promising great possibilities but fraught with great dangers. Individuals must engage themselves in reconstructionist thought. The insistence of Educational Reconstruction upon cultural transformation, involving both radical and structural changes, is exemplified by its method of working towards the goal of peace through the elimination of discrimination and oppression. Although the means may disrupt the harmony of the community, the longer range goal is that the world must renew itself. Educational Reconstructionists are, in fact, global citizens and world educators working toward a lasting peace. "Think globally and act locally," is their accepted maxim.

Freire, through his encouragement of literacy in third world countries, provides a means for meeting the crisis. Freire calls for teachers and students to reflect in small groups on their lives and the world and work together to transform it. He asks them to lead in "reading the word and the world."

Thomas examines three theoretical perspectives in dealing with the modern-world crisis. In structural functionalism, sociologists focus upon social order. They seek equilibrium. The "strain theory" of social problems, leading to crime, suicide, and violence—anomie or normlessness—calls for government interventions. However, this theory does not get to the roots.

The critical power-conflict perspective includes the contributions of Karl Marx, Ralf Dahremdorf, and C. Wright Mills. This theory focuses upon social conflict rather than upon social balance. Conflict arises through inequality and injustice stemming from power and control. Critical theorists point out that when people become literate, they recognize oppression and seek social transformation. The crisis culture wants transformation that involves fundamental or radical changes. Such changes embrace a global outlook. This perspective is more nearly in agreement with reconstructionist philosophy.

The symbolic-interaction perspective concentrates on day-to-day communication or interaction in a face-to-face situation. The Educational Reconstructionist accepts the idea of interaction and communication but sees democracy in global terms. Solutions lie in the cooperation of people everywhere.

"Engagement" is a reconstructionist concept—a belief held by people affiliated with the Society for Educational Reconstruction (SER), a formal organization founded by Brameld's students in 1969. SER attracts new members continuously. It invites new members' commitment in approaching social issues through cooperative power, global order, self-transformation, and social democracy.

The Present and Future

Darrol Bussler, in the third chapter of this volume, presents the tenets and role, the present and future, of Educational Reconstruction as one of thoughtful action in school and community. The value of this philosophy lies in its means for transmitting and transforming society, in the democratic ethic which recognizes the need for informed action for achieving agreed-upon change.

Although this philosophy borrows from others—progressive, essential, perennial perspectives—it has its own, distinctive domain which focuses upon the existential dimension of people and nature. It is a culture-based philosophy. Thus, individuals within social contexts become a major focus.

The second basic tenet is the belief that education both transmits and transforms culture, which is never static. Education modifies, changes, transforms, and reconstructs society; it builds our civilization through protecting culture while correcting, improving, and altering it by interpretation and transformation. Education does not mean indoctrination, which is the antithesis of democracy. The reconstructionist sees a democratic society as one with thinking citizens, not individuals who follow blindly, sheepishly.

Educational Reconstruction is a philosophic base for the practice of community education—schools without walls that encourage lifelong learning. It is this process which transforms the individual and society. This type of education is a basic tenet with its dual roles of transmitting and transforming social values.

Thomas and Bussler both point to the many problems facing our modern world. We are in a state of crisis. Through reconstructionist philosophy, we can rebuild our world by facing the dangers and fulfilling the potential for a new and better existence. The paradoxical meaning of crisis is made clear through our hopeful actions. We strive toward a utopia which can be realized through transformation, using non-violent means—the approach is practicing democracy. Rules for recognition of both the majority and minority are carefully defined; the idea of violent revolution is excluded from the process.

We cannot, however, solve our problems in a vacuum. We acknowledge interdependence—a common theme for reconstructionists. We must have a world-minded attitude in order "to advance mankind as a whole." With this interdependence must come international authority or world government.

The reciprocal relationship between the individual and community is also based on this theme of interdependence. Individuals reach their selves only through communication with others. We are born helpless. We achieve freedom, as a race and individuals, through the medium of culture. Individuals become conscious of their self only through being conscious of other personalities. Thus, Brameld coined the term "social-self-realization"—a form of interdependence. The powers of individuals are drawn through communion with others. Each person has one's own goals, but social-self-realization is the overarching aim which leads to the improvement and fulfillment of the world. In fashioning themselves, individuals also shape the human race and the future.

Social-self-realization means cooperative power which protects the common person. Thus, when crises arrive in our life, we struggle to overcome them. Education plays a role in the transformation of society, and the principles of democracy apply in effecting this change. Since Educational Reconstruction views necessary change as being in the core "American tradition," part of our nation's cultural roots, it can be termed radical. This radical approach focuses on the future, asking, "What kind of future? Toward what is it that reconstruction directs human energies?" The reconstructionist envisions a world of peace, brotherhood, equality, and freedom: an attainable utopia. The key word is *change*, and this philosophy gives guidance to the democratic process of change. Action must be guided by desired ends. The ends affect the functions needed to accomplish the results—Brameld's concept of ends and means.

We discover truth through thought, tested by discussion and debate, before drawing conclusions. Consensual agreement is a four-step process: presentation of evidence, communication, agreement, and action. In contrast to operational consensus is Brameld's concept of defensible partiality—comparative investigation of as many alternative approaches as are available. Once there is consensual validation, the ideas agreed upon must also be acted upon.

Value preferences become dominant goals in Educational Reconstruction, which seeks to determine universals—goals which are true for most of the people, most of the time. Brameld developed a suggested list of twelve universal goals comprising human wants. He argued that we must allow for the expression and satisfaction of the wide diversity of human want. In a continuously planning democratic society, citizens must determine the ends along with the means. Educational Reconstruction links thought with action, theory with practice. Its ultimate aim is peace, which entails well-being at both personal and societal levels. The process of transformation through action is vital to the achievement of peace—a utopian view. The philosophy is a guide to human behavior, unfinished, on-going.

Supporting Women and Minorities

As the shape of our world changes, the philosophy of Educational Reconstruction meets the demands of these transformations. Frances O'Neil, in the fourth and final chapter, discusses American minority issues, the fact that we no longer address "the" minority, but that we view various segments of our population each as "a" minority—African Americans, Hispanics, Asians, and others. The elderly and women, too, have minority voices. Social-self-realization is the foundation of Educational Reconstruction thought, which acknowledges the struggles of minority groups in overcoming prejudice and in gaining economic security within an historically, although changing, white male-dominated culture.

The pioneering efforts of women to gain recognition through the balance and maintenance of cooperative relationships and empowerment serve as a model for other striving minorities. The historically distinctly masculine bias, with its emphasis on manipulation, control, and distance from the object, is gradually changing. Objectivity is a myth, and women must liberate themselves from it, for "we are at risk when we accept 'knowledge' without examining it in its social and political context." We need more research and social action concerning the rights of women—especially women who have nevertheless sought peace for humanity through employment of the arts as agents for transforming society.

As a long-term SER member, O'Neil has gathered data about women who are active leaders in the organization. She observes social prejudice against religious commitments, the lack of an adequate voice, and a need for hard research on women's issues. SER has attempted to deal with these issues by presenting programs and fostering studies on women worldwide. In keeping with the organization's emphasis on social-self-realization, several members, including Stone and David Conrad have examined and written about women's issues.

Clearly, there is much to accomplish, not only for women, but for the other minorities as well. Educational Reconstruction is approaching these major crises through the perspectives offered—social order, critical power, conflict resolution, and constructive interaction and communication. We see the principles of Educational Reconstruction in action—transmitting worthy values and transforming the society through education. We recognize that interdependence is needed to achieve social-self-realization, and we are establishing the means to reach this desired end.

As a philosophy, Educational Reconstruction makes a valuable contribution to humanity through its advocacy of strong, well-conceived, admirable action. The test of its strength lies in the service rendered in this world of crisis. Educational Reconstruction's utopian view, accommodating a spectrum of human aspirations, keeps alive the hope for a better existence for all.

Chapter One

AGENTS OF SOCIO-EDUCATIONAL CHANGE: EDUCATIONAL RECONSTRUCTION'S ORIGINS

By Frank Andrews Stone

Theodore Brameld

A curriculum experiment was conducted at the regional high school in the rural town of Floodwood, St. Louis County, Minnesota in 1944-1945. It was initiated by Theodore Brameld, then, at the age of forty, an associate professor of educational philosophy at the University of Minnesota in Minneapolis. The juniors and seniors at the high school were involved in an integrative curriculum aimed at responding to the question: "What kind of a society do we as young citizens want to build for tomorrow?" Brameld periodically traveled over a hundred seventy miles from campus in order to participate in the cooperative thinking of these teenagers and their teachers who were exploring alternatives for the future. The outcomes of the Floodwood Project are the text of Brameld's *Design for America: An Educational Exploration of the Future of Democracy for Senior High Schools and Junior Colleges.*

Brameld was testing out his belief that a fresh outlook was needed for critical collaborative planning regarding desirable social development and progress. He argued that the strengths and weaknesses of our present social, economic, and political structures need to be re-

15

examined. Out of this analysis, convincing blue prints can be drawn up for a better cooperative order that reduces the injustices of the present system. Appropriate methods for involving students with conducting social inquiry and bringing about social change have to be devised. They need to be effective and powerful enough to reach the stated objectives. Brameld gave the name "educational reconstruction" to this intriguing philosophical process first initiated at Floodwood High School in 1944-45.[1]

This theoretical framework formed the basis of Brameld's long career as a future-oriented activist educator until his death in 1987. The way his thinking developed and his efforts to implement educational reconstruction are described in works such as *Education for the Emerging Age*, *Education as Power*, and *The Use of Explosive Ideas in Education*. He wasn't, however, content with simply formulating a philosophical position. Brameld also carried out applied field studies intended to bring reconstructionist approaches to a variety of contexts. His findings were published in *The Remaking of a Culture: Life and Education in Puerto Rico*; *Japan: Culture, Education and Change in Two Communities*; and with his wife, Midori Matsuyama, *Tourism as Cultural Learning*. These, in addition to his other writings, give readers insight into educational reconstruction as he experienced it from the mid-1940s to the late 1970s.[2]

Myles Horton

At about the same time that Brameld was experimenting with his understanding of educational reconstruction, another reconstructionist saga was unfolding in the South. Myles Horton, a native of Appalachian Tennessee, with some others, began the Highlander Folk School at Summerfield, Grundy County, Tennessee in late 1932. Although Horton died in 1990, today that tiny beginning is the Highlander Research and Education Center at New Market, Tennessee. A graduate of Cumberland University, Horton later studied with Reinhold Niebuhr at New York City's Union Theological Seminary and with sociologist Robert E. Park at the University of Chicago . He became acquainted with Jane Addam's Hull House, a settlement on Halstead Street in Chicago, that gave Horton a model for innovative education. For several months in late 1931 he was in Denmark learning about the folk schools, farmers' cooperatives, and trade unions there. All of these experiences were on Horton's mind when he began the Highlander School.

Septima Poinsette Clark, a former adult student at Highlander, found herself fired by the Charleston, South Carolina Board of Education in 1955. What was Clark's fault? Although *Brown v. Board of Education* had been handed down by the United States Supreme Court in 1953, Clark, a local black teacher, was "let go" because she was advocating school desegregation. She had been actively encouraging African Americans to qualify as voters. Even worse, in the eyes of the Board of Education, Clark had been socializing with the white judge, Waites Waring, who ruled that South Carolina had to extend the franchise to its Black citizens. She was doing all the things that had been emphasized during her stay at Highlander. Clark later became Highlander's Education Director in order to teach these values to others.

Having taught in Charleston, Septima Clark was familiar with the conditions for African Americans on Johns Island, which is nearby that city. Education was scarce, and sickness, illiteracy, and superstition were common problems. What Black schools existed on the island were dilapidated and overcrowded. Thus, generations of Johns Island adults couldn't read, write, or work the simplest arithmetic problems. They certainly couldn't read and interpret the state constitution and therefore were ineligible to register as voters. Clark brought this critical situation to Horton's attention.

Horton realized that if Highlander was to answer the plea for a "night school for adults" on Johns Island, it couldn't be in a conventional classroom. Most certified teachers didn't know the Gullah language, a dialect with traces of West African tongues, spoken by the island Blacks. Teachers would obviously have to be peers willing to show people how to read the state constitution, which was the barrier to their participating in the political process. The fact is that Horton and his White colleagues never taught in a Citizenship School, as the basic literacy programs were called. But they helped to recruit and prepare local volunteers for this role and raised the money needed in order to keep the schools going. The adults who enrolled, therefore, not only acquired literacy skills, but also learned to respect one another.

They were challenged to respond to some vital questions. Were they, as a people, responsible for their condition? Was it true that they were ignorant and unable to learn, as some people claimed? Could they accept the responsibilities of democratic decision-making and cooperative planning?

Early in 1961, the Citizenship Schools (funds, idea, support sources, and staff) were transferred to the South Christian Leadership Conference (SCLC). At that time, Highlander was facing an investigation by the Tennessee State Legislature aimed at shutting the school down, so its future was uncertain. By 1963, however, with SCLC sponsorship, Septima Clark noted that volunteers were running over 400 Citizenship Schools attended by 6,500 adults. By 1970, some 100,000 African Americans had learned functional literacy skills. Many of them succeeded in becoming registered voters in twelve Southern states where they previously were disenfranchised.

The Citizenship Schools initiated by Clark and Horton, based on the philosophy of the Highlander Folk School, illustrate the human rights and social justice aspects of Educational Reconstruction. They were intended to be the instruments of basic social change, not only in the political realm, but also in the instruction of practical skills such as map reading, interpreting road signs, dialing telephone numbers, filling out application forms, and keeping financial accounts. Adults who have these skills are empowered. At the same time, people who went to the Citizenship Schools developed respect for themselves and their culture, learned how to discuss common concerns, and how to settle disputes without violence. These are typical goals of Educational Reconstruction.[3]

Morris R. Mitchell

A third experiment with Educational Reconstruction is embodied in the life-work of Morris R. Mitchell (1895-1976). Mitchell was also a Southerner, born in Georgetown, Kentucky. His father was a higher education administrator and historian. Morris' mother, Alice Broadus Mitchell, came from a Southern Baptist background of political and religious conservatism. Yet, education was highly valued in the Mitchell household, including respect for independent thinking. Young Morris fought in World War One, a formative experience that turned him toward pacifism. As he pondered alternative means for settling international conflicts without mass destruction, Mitchell came to the conclusion that World War One and the

Great Depression of 1929-1939 had common socio-economic causes. After studying with John Dewey at Columbia University, Mitchell earned his Ph.D. at the George Peabody College for Teachers in Nashville, Tennessee in 1926.

When he had returned to America after the war, Mitchell had bought a small farm near Ellerbe, North Carolina. He planted several thousand peach trees on the land, but then needed a paid winter job. He was employed as a local school principal, and this position quickly brought him into confronting the community's social conditions which were hampering many of his students. The symptoms that Mitchell observed were "hookworm and tuberculosis, parental abuse, bad associates, overwork in the fields, ignorance in the home, low intelligence, or malnutrition."[4]

The town and school authorities, however, made no effort to track down the roots of any of these problems. Instead, the students were being labeled "discipline problems" and were frequently punished for "misbehavior." Neither they, their parents, nor the town's leaders had any long-range goals for themselves or the community.

His experience in Ellerbe led Mitchell to formulate a basic conviction that:

> education, rightly understood as a lifelong process not limited to formal schooling, could be a potentially revolutionary tool for achieving social transformation.[5]

Indeed, Mitchell liked to say that the best form of education ought to be living intelligently in community.

In 1934, Mitchell took a position in the experimental New College of Teachers College, Columbia University. He sought to pioneer the teaching of what he termed "community education." He soon was sent to Habersham County, Georgia, to work with its young school superintendent, Claude Purcell, who was trying to encourage the public school system to address community problems. Mitchell bought about a thousand acres of land outside of Clarkesville in the north Georgia hill country in the mid-1930s. Here he launched a project to apply cooperative principles in order to bring about rural re-education and revitalization. Five families were enlisted to participate in an enterprise called the "Macedonia Cooperative Association," named for a nearby Baptist Church. They bought shares and contributed their "sweat equity" to economic ventures such as lumber production, based on ecologically sound principles of forest management, and dairy farming, which required patiently rehabilitating pastureland that had been damaged. The Macedonia Cooperative also labored to improve the housing and sanitation of the involved families.

Students from the New College were frequent visitors at the Macedonia Cooperative. After 1939, Mitchell taught at the State Teachers College, Florence, Alabama, and brought his students there to see the Macedonia Project as well. It was also the location of several American Friends Service Committee summer work camps. The Macedonia Cooperative Community, however, was always underfunded. As a non-governmental operation it couldn't compete with the New Deal programs. Furthermore, when World War Two began, members of the Cooperative were attracted into Clarkesville to work at higher-paying war industries.

Macedonia survived until 1957, but by then most of the families had left the cooperative. The remaining members then decided to join the Society of Brothers (Bruderhof) which sold the property in 1958. It continues to produce a line of wooden furniture and play equipment for kindergartens and nursery schools as an appropriately non-violent means of earning an income. Although the experiment ended after some twenty years, Mitchell believed that the Macedonia Cooperative Association had developed useful operational concepts. The voluntary group had addressed some fundamental issues of production and distribution by applying democratic problem solving. The earlier Macedonia Project, in fact, is part of the inspiration for today's Koinonia Community near Americus, Georgia. It also influenced the formation of Habitat for Humanity, a Koinonia spin-off, that uses many of the same principles of Educational Reconstruction.

Mitchell wrote an article in 1947 titled, "Yes, It Can Be Done." Here he described an imaginary prototype school system at "Williston, Minnesota." The design in some ways is reminiscent of Brameld's Floodwood, Minnesota project three years earlier. Mitchell claimed:

> Activity programs have been belated efforts to relate education to making things, doing creative work, in a day when distribution, not production, is the foremost problem.... There is no one monumental, factory-like building called the School (in Williston). The campus of the school is coterminous with the community.[6]

Mitchell concluded by saying that

> The rural school of tomorrow does not exist in America today. Only fragments are to be found. Let us assemble these fragments.

Along the way, Mitchell developed a whole perspective on world education. He envisioned bringing about global peace and order through linking people together in voluntary worldwide networks. The great problems faced by all humanity would be the basis of the school curriculum. Students would actually go to the social frontiers, whether near or far, to study and to help meliorate conditions as they were occurring. The outcome of their experience would be integral, interdisciplinary knowledge replacing the artificial "egg crate" divisions of the so-called conventional disciplines and specialized fields.

Mitchell became the first president of Friends World College in Huntington, Long Island, New York in 1965 after having headed up the Putney Graduate School in Putney, Vermont. Both of these programs were innovative alternatives in higher education designed to make community internships a basic learning vehicle. Friends World College was founded by some concerned New York Quakers in order to implement the radical philosophy that Mitchell expressed in his *World Education—A Revolutionary Concept* published in 1967.[7] These ideas epitomize Educational Reconstruction and are the basis of many subsequent reconstructionist experiments. They are as fresh and timely now as when they were first written thirty years ago.

Mitchell retired from Friends World College to his cabin home in White Pines near the former Macedonia Cooperative in the North Georgia hills in 1972. This is where he died four years later at the age of eighty-three. The distinctiveness of Mitchell's career is his willingness to actually test out theories in action. He implemented ideas, involved people in reflecting on them, while critiquing and improving the concepts through application. As he stated in a personal interview toward the end of his long career:

> Educational reconstruction is best suited to the World Education movement because it has four characteristics: (1) future orientation, (2) a curriculum based on the pressing problems facing humankind, (3) a society which is ever planning (because it is ever changing), and (4) an acceptance of the problem approach.[8]

William O. Stanley

Another important source of reconstructionist ideas is William O. Stanley's *Education and Social Integration*, first published in 1953. Stanley asserted that:

> Education is more than imparting information. It is shapes and molds,...the fundamental contours of human personality—mind, conscience, interests, patterns of action and belief, even the conscious awareness of selfhood and the basic emotional structure. Education as used here refers to "the total nurture of the culture." School is only one aspect of this complex process, but it has a responsibility for the character of its charges.[9]

Stanley goes on to recognize that it is by implementing the methods of science and the social sciences that schools can involve their students and teachers in what he calls social reconstruction. There is a need, he claims, to study the salient conflicts and confusions of our times. Using diction that is familiar in Educational Reconstruction, Stanley claims that cooperative inquiry is required, leading toward operational consensus about the actions to be taken.[10]

International Roots

It should not be assumed that Educational Reconstruction is a purely American philosophy. As a matter of fact, Mohandas Karamchand Gandhi (1868-1948), the "Mahatma," very consciously carried out reconstruction in South Africa and India before the philosophy was well developed in the United States. A collection of Gandhi's articles about the Wardha Scheme for reforming the schools in 1937 is titled *Educational Reconstruction*. The complex dimensions of his thought and action have been examined, among others, by Richard Fox in *Gandhian Utopia*.[11]

The Republic of Turkey's Village Institute movement in the 1930s and 1940s, led by Ismail Hakki Tonguch, is another example of Educational Reconstruction. Tonguch's writings unfortunately haven't been translated into English, but the rationale of his work and impact of his career are examined in several journal articles. Due to the Village Institutes, a generation of rural teenagers, boys and girls, became literate and articulate. They learned about modern technology, joined the mainstream of their country, and became politically

22

conscious. Although the Village Institutes were closed by a more conservative government in the 1950s, a whole stream of Turkish writers and social reformers trace their origins to these institutions.[12]

Connecticut's Brazilian partner state in the Partners of the Americas, Paraiba, is next door to Recife, Pernambuco, where Paulo Freire initiated his program of conscientization and functional literacy in the mid-1940s. I've therefore been able to see the place where Freire and his wife, Elza, began meeting with exploited factory workers and landless farm laborers. As Freire recalls:

> I learned how to *discuss* with the people, I learned to respect their knowledge, their beliefs, their fears, their hopes, their expectations, their language. It took time and many meetings.[13]

The approach that the Freires developed is now widely known and appreciated due to the English translations of his books *Pedagogy of the Oppressed* and *Cultural Action for Freedom*. A very sophisticated method for developing adult basic literacy skills as instruments of socio-economic empowerment is presented. Although developed largely independently of European and North American theorists, in his philosophy Freire advocates Educational Reconstruction. His work embodies the reconstructionist agenda of catalyzing needed social changes through educational processes.

Philosophical Forebearers

At this point some readers are probably asking, "Didn't early Educational Reconstruction as you've described it have any forebearers?" I strongly believe that it did, but in none of them is the full philosophy of today's Educational Reconstruction to be found. One reason for this is that earlier theorists were contending with different socio-cultural and socio-economic issues than those that have faced us since the mid-twentieth century. The real world as they perceived it wasn't facing the threat of nuclear annihilation, ecological disasters, multiculturalism, and the new feminism. These are now realities that any contemporary advocate of Educational Reconstruction has to recognize. They also were not interacting with current philosophical trends such as existential thought, phenomenology, analytic theory, and critical pedagogy, as must more recent reconstructionists.

It is possible to identify in the Progressive Education and instrumentalism of John Dewey (1859-1952) some concepts that, reoriented and reinterpreted, also appear in Educational Reconstruction. Among them, for example, are the "reconstruction of human experience," emphasizing problem solving by applying scientific methods, using democratic processes, and making "warranted assumptions." The question about how much Educational Reconstruction owes to its antecedents, however, was raised forty-five years ago in 1951. Then and now, after recognizing some influence, the conclusion is that reconstruction significantly differs from progressivism in its premises, methods, and applications.[14]

I believe that W.E.B. DuBois (1868-1963) is much more a true forbearer of Educational Reconstruction. DuBois' famous field study of African Americans in the "City of Brotherly Love" in 1896-1898, that is the basis of his *The Philadelphia Negro,* is one of the first efforts to apply ethnography in order to bring about needed social changes. As one of his biographers writes, DuBois faced a conundrum familiar to social scientists with commitments to Educational Reconstruction. He had to write what amounted to two books in one:

> —one that would not be immediately denounced or ridiculed by the arbiters of mainstream knowledge, influence, and order for its transparent heterodoxy; and a second one that would, over time, deeply penetrate the social sciences and gradually improve race-relations policy through its not-immediately apparent interpretive radicalism. He set about, then, to write a study affirming and modifying, yet also significantly subverting the received sociological wisdom of the day.[15]

DuBois' work that anticipates Educational Reconstruction includes his Atlanta University Studies, an annual research series issued after 1897. These were the intellectual grist for the Atlanta Conferences of Negro Problems. Among them were "The Negro Artisan" (1902), "The Negro Church" (1903), and especially "The Negro American Family" (1908). He had authored studies in 1900 and 1901 on Blacks in the colleges and public schools. These were replicated and expanded in 1910 and 1911 as "The College-bred Negro" and "The Negro Common School." DuBois' conclusion to the latter report states that:

> Race antagonism can only be stopped by intelligence. It is dangerous to wait, it is foolish to hesitate. Let the nation immediately give generous aid to Southern common school education.[16]

This unfortunately didn't happen, but imagine how much better subsequent events might have been if DuBois' call for funding school desegregation had received an adequate response at that time.

The terms of three centuries of Black/White relationships were redefined in DuBois' *The Souls of Black Folk*, originally published in 1903. Its fourteen essays were:

> ...an electrifying manifesto, mobilizing a people for bitter prolonged struggle to win a place in history. Ironically, even its author was among the tens of thousands whose conceptions of themselves were to be forever altered by the book.[17]

It isn't feasible to recount here DuBois' roles in the Niagara Movement or the Pan-African Congress held in Paris, France in 1919. Nor can his work as the founding editor of *The Crisis*, journal of the National Association for the Advancement of Colored People (NAACP), be examined. Our conclusion must be, however, that DuBois gives us a model of someone implementing the philosophical principles that were later known as Educational Reconstruction. The careers of many other reconstructionists have followed in his footsteps.

The Social Frontier

The historian Merle Curti has pointed out that as early as 1922 George Counts was drawing attention to shortcomings in the existing socio-economic structures. Counts, who was a professor at Teachers College, Columbia University, claimed that American industry was inefficient and wasteful. Employees' incomes were not only grossly unequal, but in many cases insufficient to provide a decent standard of living. This was certainly true in many American cities and parts of Appalachia. Another huge social problem, as Counts saw it, was that wealth and power were distributed in ways that were neither economically nor ethically justified. The public schools, he believed, had been coopted into helping to maintain this condition of privilege for a few under the guise of being democratic institutions.

Counts' research and the writing based on his studies are clearly pioneer works of Educational Reconstruction. He wrote, for example, an article in 1922 on "The Selective Character of American Secondary Education." His monograph about *The Social Composition of Boards of Education* that demonstrated how they were controlled by elites in many communities came out in 1927. Counts' famous pamphlet entitled *Dare the School Build a New Social Order?* was issued in 1932. This is a seminal work of Educational Reconstruction which Counts himself acknowledged by joining the Society for Educational Reconstruction soon after it was founded in 1969.[18]

It was a small journal called *The Social Frontier* published by a few activist educators, primarily associated with Teachers College, Columbia University that carried articles by George Counts and like-minded writers. Among them was Harold Rugg, author of works such as *Culture and Education in America* (1931), and *The Great Technology*, (1933). Another of *The Social Frontier* writers was Brameld, whom we have already observed carrying out the Floodwood Project in Minnesota.

To Bring about Change

By the 1920s, most of American Progressive Education had been domesticated. It had become a mild approach for reforming curriculum and instructional methodology in the schools. But this philosophy of education didn't address the critical social issues of the day, such as the lack of basic civil rights for people of color. It had little to say about the unhealthy growth of industry in Appalachia initiated by and paid for by outside corporations. These developments had made the local people simply "hired hands" dependent on corporate policy for their wages and working conditions. The public schools conformed to racial segregation and did little to prepare students to engage in social planning or devise strategies for bringing about change. As the Great Depression, many subsequent economic recessions, and a series of wars unfolded, it has been the philosopher-activists of Educational Reconstruction who tried to address these issues. This has been the socio-economic ground from which today's Educational Reconstruction grew.

Discussion Suggestions

To further explore your understanding of the history of Educational Reconstruction, try the following suggestions for discussion:

1. Imagine that Theodore Brameld, Myles Horton and Morris Mitchell are having a conversation about education and social change in the twenty-first century. What do you think their priorities would

be? Which problems would most concern them? What would likely be their design for a sustainable and fulfilling global society? Critique what you believe their perspectives would be on Educational Reconstruction in the twenty-first century by presenting your own viewpoint.

2. Carol Jago, an English teacher at Santa Monica High School wrote these thoughts for the *Los Angeles Times*:

> An adversarial relationship between those who teach and those who learn only reinforces children's notion that assignments are purposely confusing and textbooks purposefully obscure. Drivers know that a road map was created to help them get from Point A to Point B. No one believes that a conspiracy of cartographers lurks behind every page. But too often, children believe that teachers create assignments simply to trip them up.
>
> What students miss is the big picture. Few have been asked to think deeply about why they spend all this time in school. What do they hope to accomplish in a particular year, in a particular class? How can they reach these goals? What skills do they need that they haven't yet acquired?
>
> Students follow a plan for kindergarten, primary school, junior high and high school because they have no choice, without ever generating an educational vision of their own. Lacking direction, these children founder. They become frustrated when, after going through all the motions of traditional schooling, they are told that intellectually they still come up short.
>
> I know the feeling. It's what happens to me behind the wheel. Without a clear idea of where I'm going, I misread one sign and am hopelessly lost.[19]

Is Jago discussing Educational Reconstruction? Do you recognize any reconstructionist themes in her essay? What aspects of her position aren't consonant with Educational Reconstruction? Why?

3. Draw up a preliminary blueprint for change and development in your community or neighborhood during the next five years. Identify those movements that you think are near certain to happen, the interventions that people could make if they wished, and the goals toward which it would be desirable to work. Can you devise any appropriate methods or strategies for influencing change and development in your locality? What options and alternatives do people your age have in the social situation as you see it?

4. Peter Applebome, national education reporter for *The New*

York Times, in an article on teacher preparation in the "Education Life" section identifies four issues that are currently being debated:

Diversity. There are widespread concerns about how to prepare an overwhelmingly white teaching corps for an increasingly minority student population, and how to recruit more members of minorities to the profession.

Curriculum. Educators are debating how college students' time should be divided among taking the subjects they plan to teach, learning about teaching, and being a student teacher. They also debate whether it makes sense to add a fifth year to the curriculum devoted almost solely to teaching.

Collaboration. There is broad support for creating partnerships between education schools and public schools to build so-called professional development schools, which would function the way teaching hospitals do for doctors. Only a few such schools are operating.

Technology. Many agree that teachers need to be better prepared to adapt to new technologies, particularly computers, but barriers—in costs and expertise—remain.

What links all the issues is a problem with no easy solution: how to bridge the chasm between elementary and secondary schools that distrust university schools of education and universities that generally look down on their own education schools as insufficiently rigorous trade schools.[20]

Bringing to bear your knowledge of the origins of Educational Reconstruction, what do you believe this philosophy has to say on these matters? Is Educational Reconstruction, in your judgment, timely and effective today in light of the current crises in the real world?

Notes

1. Theodore Brameld, *Design for America: An Educational Exploration of the Future of Democracy for Senior High Schools and Junior Colleges.* An American Education Fellowship Book. New York: Hinds, Hayden and Eldredge, Inc., 1945. See also Craig Kridel, "Theodore Brameld's Floodwood Project: A Design for America," in Frank Andrews Stone, editor, *Educational Reconstruction*, An Anthology 1974-1978 from *Cutting Edge: Journal of the Society for Educational Reconstruction.*

Storrs, CT: Parousia Press, 1978, 81-90.
2. Theodore Brameld, *Education for the Emerging Age: Newer Ends and Stronger Means*. New York: Harper and Row, 1950, 1961, 1965. Theodore Brameld, *Education as Power*. New York: Holt, Rinehart and Winston, 1965. Theodore Brameld, *The Use of Explosive Ideas in Education: Culture, Class and Evolution*. Pittsburgh, PA: University of Pittsburgh Press, 1965. Theodore Brameld, *The Remaking of a Culture: Life and Education in Puerto Rico*. New York: John Wiley and Sons, 1959. Theodore Brameld, *Japan: Culture, Education and Change in Two Communities*. New York: Holt, Rinehart and Winston, 1968. Theodore Brameld and Midori Matsuyama, *Tourism as Cultural Learning: Two Controversial Case Studies in Educational Anthropology*. Washington, DC: University Press of America, 1977.
3. Frank Adams, *Unearthing Seeds of Fire: The Idea of Highlander*. Winston-Salem, NC: John F. Blair, Publisher, 1975. Brenda Bell, Gohn Gaventa, and John Peters, editors, *We Make the Road by Walking: Conversations on Education and Social Change, Myles Horton, and Paulo Freire*. Philadelphia, PA: Temple University Press, 1990. There is a selected bibliography on Myles Horton, XXXVI-XXXVII. Myles Horton, with Judith and Herbert Kohl, *The Long Haul: An Autobiography*. New York: Doubleday, 1990. Myles Horton participated in a "Hardscrabble Seminar" with the members of the Society for Educational Reconstruction at Theodore Brameld's home in Lyme, NH in the mid-1970's.
4. W. Edward Orver, "Morris R. Mitchell (1895-1976): Social and Educational Visionary," *Appalachian Journal: A Regional Studies Review* 4(2), Winter, 1977, 100-104. See also Bart Sobel, "A Tribute to a World Educator: Morris Randolph Mitchell, 1895-1976," reprinted from the *Journal of World Education*.
5. *Ibid.*
6. Morris R. Mitchell, "Yes, It Can Be Done," *Progressive Education*, January, 1947, 88, 109.
7. Morris Mitchell, *World Education—Revolutionary Concept*. New York: Pageant Press, 1967.
8. Bart Sobel, "World Education in Light of Four Educational Philosophies," in *Educational Reconstruction, an Anthology*, 1974-1978, 91-96.
9. William O. Stanley, *Education and Social Integration*. New York: Teachers College Press, 1953, seventh printing, 1969, 119.
10 *Ibid.*, 255.
11. Mohandas K. Gandhi, *Educational Reconstruction*, Sixth Edition. Sevagram, India: Hindustani Talimi Sangh, 1956. Richard G. Fox, *Gandhian Utopia: Experiments with Culture*. Boston, MA: Beacon Press, 1989.

12. Frank A. Stone, "A Pioneer in Turkish Village Revitalization." *Hacettepe Bulletin of the Social Sciences and Humanities* 2(2), 1970, 220-234. Frank A. Stone, "Rural Revitalization and the Village Institutes of Turkey: Sponsors and Critics," *Comparative Education Review*, 18(3), 1974, 419-429.

13. Bell, *et. al.*, editors, *We Make the Road*, 65. See xxv-xxxvi for a selected bibliography of eight of Freire's works and four analyses of his theories and career.

14. E. Sayers, "Is Reconstructionism a Flowering of Progressivism?" *Educational Theory*, 1, 1951, 211-217.

15. David Levering Lewis, *W.E.B. DuBois: Biography of a Race, 1868-1919.* New York: Henry Holt and Company, 1993, 189.

16. *Ibid.*, 221.

17. *Ibid.*, 277.

18. Merle Curti, *The Social Ideas of American Educators*, New and Revised Edition. Totowa, NJ: Littlefield, Adams and Company, 1966 (original, 1935), 568-572.

19. Carol Jago, "Help Children Map Their Own Futures in School," *The Hartford Courant*, January 3, 1996.

20. Peter Applebome, "Is Experience the Best Teacher: Debating almost everything about how to train new educators," *The New York Times*, "Education Life," Section 4-A, January 7, 1996, 22-24.

A Short Bibliography of Current Materials on Educational Reconstruction

Books

Aberley, Doug, editor. *Futures by Design: The Practice of Ecological Planning*. Philadelphia, PA: New Society Publishers, 1994. 214 pp. $14.95

Beare, Hedley, & Richard Slaughter. *Education for the Twenty-First Century*. New York: Rutledge, 1993. 180 pp. $14.95

Boulding, Elise. *Building a Global Civic Culture: Education for an Interdependent World*. Syracuse, NY: Syracuse University Press, 1990. 176 pp. $12.95

Cashman, Sean, editor. *Healing the Heart of Cities: Young Voices Speak Out*. Washington, DC: Campus Outreach Opportunity League, 1995. 91 pp. free. (COOL, 1511 K Street, N.W., #307, Washington, D.C. 20005, 202/637-7004)

Gang, Philip, Nina Meyerhof Lynn, & Dorothy Maver. *Conscious Education: The Bridge to Freedom*. Chamblee, GA: Dagaz Press, 1995. $17.45 (Dagaz Press, P.O. Box 80651, Chamblee, GA, 30366)

Hollender, Jeffrey. *How to Make the World a Better Place: 116 Ways You Can Make a Difference.* New York: W.W. Norton, 1995. 284 pp. $13.00

James, Michael E., editor. *Social Reconstruction through Education: The Philosophy, History, and Curricula of a Radical Ideal.* Social and Policy Issues in Education: The David C. Anchin Series. Norwood, NJ: Ablex Publishing Corporation, 1995. 172 pp., indices. ISBN 1-56750-145-1. Contains seven essays by Michael W. Apple, James M. Giarelli, James Wallace, Peter Carbone and Virginia Wilson, Susan Semel, Michael James, and William O. Stanley and Kenneth D. Beene.

Kaner, Sam; with Lenny Lind, Duane Berger, Catherine Toldi & Sarah Fisk. *Building Consensus in Groups: Putting Participatory Values into Practice.* Philadelphia, PA: New Society Publishers, 1996. 224 pp. $1995.

Oliner, Pearl I. & Samuel P. *Toward a Caring Society: Ideas into Action.* Westport, CT: Greenwood Publishing Group,1995. 256 pp. $19.95. (Greenwood Publishing Group, P.O. Box 5007, Westport, CT 06881)

Reardon, Betty. *Educating for Human Dignity: Learning about Rights and Responsibilities.* Baltimore, MD: University of Pennsylvania Press, 1995. $27.45. (University of Pennsylvania Press, P.O. 4836, Hampden Station, Baltimore, MD 21211)

Ruggiero, Greg, & Stuart Sahulka, editors. *The New American Crisis: Radical Analyses of the Problems Facing America Today.* New York: The New Press, 1995. 327 pp. $13.95. Twenty-two articles by Cornel West, bell hooks, Howard Zinn, David Dellinger, and Manning Marable, among others.

Seeger, Peter. *Where Have All The Flowers Gone: A Singer's Stories, Songs, Seeds, Robberies.* A "Musical Autobiography." Bethlehem, PA: Sing Out Publications, 1993. 292 pp. $17.95. (Sing Out Publications, Box 5253, Bethlehem, PA 18015, 215/865-5366).

Stanley, William B. *Curriculum for Utopia: Social Reconstructionism and Critical Pedagogy in the Postmodern Era.* Albany, NY: State University of New York Press, 1992.

Teaching for Real Change: Best Books and Resources. Cambridge: MA: Educators for Social Responsibility, 1994. 80 pp. $12.00. (Educators for Social Responsibility, 23 Graden Street, Cambridge, MA 02138, 800/370-2515)

Thomas, T.M., David R. Conrad, & Gertrude F. Langsam, editors. *Global Images of Peace and Education: Transforming the War System.* Ann Arbor: MI: Prakken Publications, Inc., 1987. 276 pp. $15.00. (Currently out-of-print, use library copies.)

Periodicals

Democratic Culture Newsletter. Teachers for a Democratic Culture, P.O. Box 6405, Evanston, IL 60204.

EarthRoots: News and Views of Grassroots Activists. EarthRoots, P.O. Box 261, Southbury, CT 06488. Published every six weeks, $12/year.

Harmony: Voices for a Just Future. An Independent Journal Promoting a Consistent Ethic of Reverence for Life. Special issue on books, journals, magazines and videos. February, 1996, 24 pp., #2. Sea Fog Press, Inc., P.O. Box 210056, San Francisco, CA 94121.

Peacework: Global Thought and Local Action for Nonviolent Social Change. Eleven issues/year, $15. Peacework, American Friends Service Committee, 2161 Massachusetts Avenue, Cambridge, MA 02140, 617/661-6130.

SER in Action! Quarterly newsletter, $25/year. The Society for Educational Reconstruction. 600 University Avenue, Room 215, Bridgeport, CT 06601.

Teaching for Change Newsletter. $15/year. Network of Educators on the Americas (NECA). 1118 22nd Street, N.W., Washington, D.C. 20037, 202/429-0137.

Booklets

Coalition for Cooperative Community Economics. TRANET, P.O. Box 567, Rangeley, ME 04970. (207)864-2252. Presents a series of "how-to-do-it" procedures for social innovations that empower people and promote community self-reliance. $1 each.

Chapter Two

Social Problems and Issues:
Views of an Educational Reconstructionist

By T. Mathai Thomas

Introduction

"What is the major problem in America today that disturbs you most?" My class in philosophy of education begins with this question or a similar one dealing with the present social condition. Instead of selecting from a list of problems which the students are familiar with, I want them to choose one which is of most concern to them personally. Most students in my class last year answered violence (fighting, crime, indiscipline). During my visit to India last year, I asked the same type of question in some colleges where I gave lectures. The answer I received was corruption (bureaucracy, bribery, political dishonesty). In my teaching, I have always been interested in finding out the views of students regarding the social conditions of the times and their concerns and commitment for social change.

I have been teaching at the University of Bridgeport since 1969, the year that the Society for Educational Reconstruction (SER) was formed. I came here after teaching high school biology in India for ten years and in two American colleges for five years. I have taught courses not only in the field of education, but also in the departments of sociology, psychology, and philosophy. The one course I have repeatedly taught over three decades has been philosophy of educa-tion. Each year I modify the course, select new readings, and keep it up-to-date. Of course, there have been core topics and themes over the years. During all of these years, my course in philosophy of education has encouraged students to look at the world in a different light from their familiar way of doing so. Hence a discussion of social issues and problems has been maintained. Now, looking back, I see that my rationale, as well as my pattern of teaching, is related to educational reconstruction.

Major Social Problems of the Last Three Decades and Earlier

We have already noted that violence is the leading social problem selected by my students in recent years. When I started my college teaching in America during the mid 1960s, the major problems seen by my students were racial discrimination, busing, and poverty. In the next decade, the 1970s, a few new problems emerged—environment, pollution, and gender inequality. The 1980s witnessed a shift in social trends and my students pointed to the widening of the gap between the rich and the poor. The idea of equality slowly yielded to the attraction of excellence and the rise of elites. Also, my students' perceptions on war took a definite shape following the Vietnam War and the huge expenditures for weapons since the "Cold War." Students identified the dangers of war as the number-one problem of the mid 1980s, followed by drug use and other destructive behaviors. The end of the Cold War reduced weapons manufacture and changed the economic situation. Now my students see the problems of the early 1990s to be unemployment and financial insecurity. Society has been guided by immediate gratification and easy money-making. People have resorted to violence and crime to fulfill their hopes and dreams.

This summary of social problems during the last thirty years, noting a few key issues from each decade, will perhaps not be meaningful to readers who are looking for a comprehensive review. Since I cannot undertake such a task in this chapter, let me try to present these issues in a larger context. The decade of the 1960s, however unique or distinct from other periods, must be seen in relation to earlier events and trends of American history.

The United States of America was not a "major power" even at the beginning of the 20th century. However, its identity as a nation with a distinct or unique character had emerged by this time, as a result of the process of Americanization starting with independence in 1776. The vision of a new nation was expressed in the famous Declaration of Independence through the ideals of equality (all human beings are created equal), life, liberty, and the pursuit of happiness. People who had reached the "new" land from many lands and cultures, initially living in thirteen diverse colonies, emerged as a nation for a new experiment in living, best described by the idea called democracy.

The 19th century was then a period of stabilization, of becoming "American," of developing a sense of oneness out of pluribus, and of growth and expansion into a vast area of land. The "Frontier Spirit" of those who dared to enter into the unknown gave shape to American character. For America, the 19th century was one of transition in pursuit of "progress," and this transition involved the beginning of a shift from a rural-agricultural life to an urban-industrial life.

At the beginning of the 20th century (soon after 1910) more people worked in manufacturing than in farming. Progressive ideas flourished at this time in various ways, including education. However, the Great Depression followed in the 1930s, and the resulting scarcity and need to stand in line for basic necessities of life shaped another side of the American character, already known for its helping hand and voluntary services. The Second World War changed everything, and a super power was born through rapid American growth and expansion during a short period of time. In the 1940s and 1950s, people enjoyed the fruits of prosperity as the nation expanded all social institutions, especially education. In such a context the growth of a counter culture might not be expected, but it happened in the 1960s.

Let me conclude this section by reiterating that the style of my teaching of philosophy of education involves selecting the major social problems and issues of the day. I have here presented two or three such problems for each decade. To make them more meaningful, I have described the last three decades in the larger context of American history. I admit that there are other major social issues not covered in this "skeletal" discussion. I am aware that I have not mentioned the population problem, technological issues, health-related questions, and gender discrimination. My purpose is not to prepare a comprehensive list of issues, but rather to show that philosophy of education can be taught by identifying social problems and issues of our times. Today this approach seems to have wider appeal than a "school of thought" approach in which some six or seven "systems" of philosophy of education were studied. As a class discusses social issues, major differences in perspective appear, because some individuals look at social conditions in a conservative mode while others do so from a liberal or radical position. One will assume education to be the transmission of culture, while the another sees education as a transformation. To me, education must transform the culture. Why? My reasons, first personal and second professional, are noted below.

Rationale for Teaching: Personal Level

We must have reasons for the things we are doing. Since our job or career is often most important among all our activities, our reasons for continuing the career determine the quality of our living. "He who has a *why* to live can bear with almost any *how*." This famous aphorism of Nietzsche seems to be the theme of Neil Postman's recent book, *The End of Education: Redefining the Value of School*. Postman makes a plea for seeking the reasons for our schooling—indeed, the purposes or ends of education. He calls it the metaphysical side of education, which he argues must be placed above the "engineering" or "technical" side to which we give priority in our schools today. There are both personal and professional reasons for my teaching that agree with the educational philosophy of Reconstructionism.

There are at least three reasons for my adherence to the philosophy of Educational Reconstruction. They are: (1) My studies at a small graduate school in Putney, Vermont, directed by Morris Mitchell; (2) My association with Theodore Brameld, my major adviser during doctoral studies at Boston University; and (3) A network of friends committed to the same philosophy, starting at Boston University and growing during all the years since.

I came to the United States from India in 1963 for my second Masters Degree, to be taken from Putney Graduate School, a very small experimental educational institution located in rural Putney,

Vermont. I had had ten years of teaching experience at one high school, a career I started in Kerala, India, at the age of twenty. I reached a new and strange land in every respect. There were no friends awaiting me, no familiar behavior patterns to assist me, and little knowledge of this strange graduate school. Putney Graduate School had about ten to fifteen students at one time, all studying for a Masters Degree in one year after going through a very unusual program. A typical day consisted of a morning seminar and afternoon work, such as making a special chair with a frame and leather upholstery. All students and teachers (Mitchell and two assistants) stayed in two buildings, working and also cooking together. This "typical" day was a rare experience, as it turned out, because we actually spent most of the time "on the road" in a van visiting places and learning together.

For example, during my second week at the school, we visited Harlem, New York, to study the condition of the poor by staying in the area for about a week and by associating with and working with some voluntary organizations which provided us accommodation. This participant observation was very effective because we were also equally sharing a "culture of poverty" with people in the Harlem area. We visited New York three or four times during the year to study city planning (conferences with city planning officials), the United Nations (meeting foreign dignitaries), and education (visiting the Bronx High School of Science and Lincoln High School for a study in contrast). During this one year of study we also visited distant social projects such as the Tennessee Valley Authority (to see its huge dams and study depression-era programs), strip mining in the South (an environmental issue before anyone recognized it as a social problem), the Southern Christian Leadership Conference (attending leadership meetings for a voter registration drive), and the Highlander Research Center (a good model of community education directed by Myles Horton). The stay at all these places was very "comfortable" because we carried our sleeping bags to make our own bed on a nice floor. Also, there were several one-day visits to nearby places in Vermont and neighboring states in order to see schools and colleges with innovative programs, "half-way houses," state mental hospitals, and other centers with creative ideas in action.

The last three months in the nine-month study program at this school were set apart for doing a project which the student devised under Mitchell's guidance. In my case, I planned a tour of America by Greyhound Bus—ninety-nine days for $99.00. I covered many cities in the East, West, North, and South, visiting the most interesting places and events. Everywhere I visited I stayed with American families, for two or three days in each city as arranged by "Servas," an organization for foreign visitors that helps them to travel and to promote an international outlook. The visits were so fascinating and "eventful" that I invariably find that one or two stories from this trip get shared with my classes every semester.

I openly admire the Putney Graduate School as the best example of Educational Reconstruction in practice. The key person in conducting such a program was Mitchell, who started the school about a decade before my arrival there. He had the assistance of two persons, one especially for tour arrangements. Mitchell had great visions on education as it relates to community and showed new dimensions of this vision in action. It gave me new perceptions by opening up higher horizons of education.

My study at Putney Graduate School took place during the last year of that school (1963-64) because it then merged with Antioch College, another experimental institution in higher education. Mitchell then left, and the school changed from its previous character which I describe here. In my case, I made my move from Putney to Boston, from the practice of Educational Reconstruction to its study under its chief theoretician. The Putney Graduate School had been guided by the writings of Brameld, especially his volume, *Toward a Reconstructed Philosophy of Education*, the "Bible" of the Putney program.

Mitchell introduced me to Brameld. This was more than a simple introduction, because he did his best to make possible my continued study at Boston University with Brameld, or Ted, as I came to know him. Indeed, I was the first and only person from the Putney Graduate School during its existence of ten or twelve years to go on to study educational reconstruction in depth for a doctorate degree. One fine morning, Morris took the phone and dialed Ted in Boston. Before mentioning any name, Morris asked the question, "Is this the greatest educational philosopher on earth?" Even today, I do not know what Ted's answer was. You may think that Morris was eccentric; yes, he was, just as any creative person is. In my case, I knew that I would find a friend in Ted just as Morris had been my close friend. Indeed, Brameld was not only a great teacher to me, but also a close associate for three years during my studies at Boston University and for another twenty years until his death in 1987.

I started my studies at Boston University in 1964 under Brameld's guidance. He was the leading philosopher of Educational Reconstruction in the world. Since he was going to Japan for one year to study Japanese culture (1964-65), he asked me to take courses with Kenneth Benne and Paul Nash, two outstanding scholars whose philosophies were not very different from Brameld's. The first course I took with Ted was on Japanese culture, a new course that he had developed. I studied not only this one culture, but educational anthropology in general. I learned that educational philosophy needs a "culturological approach," as Brameld advocated. I do not, however, like some of his specialized terms and his "more than complex" sentences, just as I disagreed with Ted on religious faith perspectives. But these differences did not stand in the way of our teacher-student relationship or friendship.

Brameld taught me how to look at the world with its problems and prospects. The term he used was "crisis," a term conveying two opposing or paradoxical meanings: one of great possibilities, and the other of real dangers. Our modern world is in crisis, and hence we must rebuild it to avoid the dangers, or problems, as well as to fulfill its potential. We can strive to achieve a paradise which people could only dream about in the past. Brameld was really committed to building a new world, and he formulated new concepts and ideas for achieving his goal.

There were several students who were fascinated by Brameld's ideas and philosophy of Educational Reconstruction. They developed a circle of friendship informally during their student life in Boston and eventually a formal organization by the fall of 1969 with the name The Society for Educational Reconstruction (SER). These students soon became professors at different colleges and universities in this country and around the world, and they have maintained their contacts in various ways. Once SER was an organization, formal meetings were arranged from time to time, and journals and books were published. In addition, SER members regularly have attended national meetings of larger educational organizations which maintain a liberal outlook and have arranged SER sessions on timely topics.

In my case, I cherish this circle of SER friends from whom I have learned much. Recently, I find some of my students taking an interest in SER activities, so I work closely with them. In these intimate relationships, education flowers and bears fruit. Given the overly formalized organization of education during our modern period, something valuable is being lost—namely, the closeness of people. The traditional practice of education during ancient times in India is known for its close teacher-pupil relationship. The system by which the student stayed with the *Guru* (great teacher), in the home or hermitage, as a member of the family, is known as *Gurukula*. Both teachers and students have mutual obligations or duties to fulfill beyond conveying information. Though the system has disappeared over the years, a special quality in the teacher-pupil relationship prevails, with a sense of respect or reverence toward a learned person. On my visits to India, I always arranged a meeting with my first-grade teacher at her house in our village, until her death in 1995. I feel fortunate that I continued similar close teacher-pupil relations with my professors in America, which, along with other Western nations, is known for its impersonal relations.

I can say, in short, that I am proud of my philosophy of Educational Reconstruction which I owe to the influences of Mitchell, Brameld, and the SER circle of friends with whom I keep up close relationships. Because of the influence of these people, I am able to see social problems in a certain perspective and work to change the world for the better. What is special about this perception and why and how do we work for a better world? To seek the answer, at least my answer, let us turn to the next section—from the personal to the professional.

Teaching Philosophy of Education in Reconstructionist Perspectives

We mentioned previously that most instructors in philosophy of education today follow a social issues approach. There are significant differences among them, because some of them stand for transmitting a culture while others are for transforming it. To Brameld, there are four "culturological approaches" to philosophy of education: (1) Cultural transmission in Essentialism (transmit the values and knowledge of the past, prevailing in the modern culture); (2) Cultural restoration in Perennialism (restore or resurrect the spirit and principles of an earlier period, such as the Middle Ages); (3) Cultural moderation in Progressivism (moderate or evolutionary changes for social reforms and progress); and (4) Cultural transformation in Reconstructionism (transform social institutions by radical and structural changes to build a better world). In addition, philosophy of education courses usually include two more contemporary approaches: (1) Philosophic analysis; and (2) Existentialism.

What is the distinctive approach of Educational Reconstructionism in dealing with social issues? Let us take the issue of war and peace as an illustration. Everyone is for peace, regardless of different philosophic orientations. However, there is a fundamental difference when we explain what peace means and how it is achieved. A conservative wants to maintain peace and order in a community without disrupting its harmony, even if peace involves discrimination, racial and gender bias, and other social ills. In the 1960s, southern states in the United States considered the Civil Rights Movement to be threatening the peace which they had kept too long. In this situation, a liberal advocated changes in racial discrimination, but as a gradual process, perhaps with more trade schools and technical education. But a radical stand emerged from some people, advocating integrated schools, voting rights, and desegregated public places. No doubt, the immediate result involved conflicts and fights between blacks and whites. Reconstructionists expect and support such conflicts because they lead to structural changes and secure a just peace. Hence, peace is more than maintaining social harmony. Rather, it is the process of eliminating discrimination and oppression (racial in this case) in order to achieve social well-being that is rooted in equality and justice.

Another distinctive approach of Educational Reconstruction is its global orientation. Increasingly we recognize that the problems we face in our surroundings are global in scope. For example, the damage inflicted on the environment affects people everywhere on earth regardless of nation or region. Ozone depletion can destroy planet Earth and all forms of life in it. Other problems, such as overpopulation, are regarded as national concerns, but common efforts by all nations to study the seriousness of the situation and to find solutions are on the rise. In this recognition of the global dimension of social problems, advocates of reconstruction have been ahead of others. Mitchell and Brameld, two leading reconstructionists of the past generation, lived their lives as "world educators" and "global citizens." They were ahead of their times in anticipating the nature of an emerging age. Today people admit the interdependence of our "global village" where our survival depends on cooperation; if we do not stand together, we will be destroyed separately.

A third distinctiveness of the philosophy in handling problems is its action orientation. A favorite theme or motto of Educational Reconstructionism is "Think globally and act locally." With a global outlook, people are encouraged to take action in changing the "world." It is not just the local community that is improving, but, in a way, the whole world. Following the writings of John Dewey, it is Paulo Freire who in the last two or three decades has given philosophic contributions to the notion of action, or "praxis." Through his encouragement of adult literacy in Third World countries, Freire helps in "reading the word and the world." Today illiteracy is still a major problem of many countries. When people learn to read they also change the world for the better because of the informed decisions that are possible on the part of a literate person. Today the members of the Society for Educational Reconstruction are actively involved in solving local problems. These activities keep the group together as both scholars and activists.

Let me conclude this section by emphasizing that I have not presented a comprehensive list reflecting the distinctiveness of Educational Reconstruction in dealing with social problems. Rather, I have tried to show that among various philosophies of education, Reconstructionism, to me, is most suitable for knowing and for acting on social problems. Its unique approach to problems and issues of our times is increasingly relevant because of the "crisis" nature of our culture, a term indicating both dangers and possibilities. It is possible to build a "utopia," the best world that people in the past only could dream. However, we have to overcome the dangers, the destruction of planet Earth. Students must be challenged with this great choice so that we can win their support and commitment in building a better world. If worthwhile commitments are not built early in life, young people may well fall victim to the immediate gratification goals that are so plentiful in our world today. It is time to look beyond, to a better future, and continue our journey to accomplish the "good life" for all human beings, those living today and coming tomorrow on this planet Earth.

Theoretical Orientations

A scientific study of social problems in a society is within the province of the discipline sociology, which involves "the scientific study of human social life." Sociologists have formulated theoretical positions in their study of society or human beings in groups both big (macro) and small (micro). They take special interest in the study of social problems because in so doing there is the potential for knowing more about human interaction in groups, the focus of sociology. I believe that our discussion of social problems, as we deal with them in our every day living, can be enriched by making use of the theories developed by sociologists.

People observe and interpret social events and trends in various ways. The questions we raise influence the explanation we reach regarding any social phenomenon. The different types of questions that a person is likely to ask reflect his or her theoretical orientation. A working set of assumptions or perspectives is brought to light in any theory.

Theorizing is the attempt to get a synoptic vision of some subject matter. The word "theory," from its Greek roots, means a vantage point, as on a high hill or on a reviewing podium as a parade passes by. It does not necessarily mean seeing everything at once, but rather seeing things in connection, the whole of the action as it happens, the whole army as it passes by. In philosophy, the Greek root means continuous and connected exposition, so that the argument is run through and tied together. Scientific theory is a special sub-code of the more general notion of theory because it focuses on explanation of phenomena.

We have noted that social scientists, especially sociologists, see social problems from different perspectives. Hence, the questions they raise and the answers they receive are brought together in various categories. Here we select three theoretical orientations widely used in sociology.

(1) Structural-Functionalism

In this perspective the focus is on social order and its persistence in society. A society is seen as an organized structure or network of groups operating in an orderly manner according to a set of rules and values shared by most members. Each group, or even institution, fulfills certain functions for social equilibrium and since each part persists, we consider it "functional."

Most sociologists in the mainstream have been primarily concerned with social order both in Europe and America. Emile Durkheim (1858-1917), a French sociologist, directed his attention to the issue of social integration brought to capitalistic society by an increasing division of labor. He developed a "strain theory" of social problems and discussed the strains in societies that he thought led to the social problems of crime, suicide, and violence. In this view, the breakdown of traditional organization, as in the presumed loss of respect for traditional authority, led to a breakdown of accepted standards and values, what he called *anomie* or normlessness. This explanation of social problems received wide acceptance in America, especially among early sociologists (Feagin, 1986, pp. 11-14).

In America, Talcott Parsons (1902-1979), following the Durkheimian tradition, focused on social order and corporate liberalism which advocated government intervention to help corporations make a profit and to reduce workers' protests when necessary, thus resolving conflict within the framework of capitalism. The book *Contemporary Social Problems* (1971), written by Parsons' student, Robert Merton has been most influential in America and elsewhere during the last two or three decades. In this book, a social problem is defined as a behavior pattern regarded by a large part of a society as "being in violation of one or more generally accepted or approved norms." These theorists do not support "a total change of society" for solving social problems.

For advocates of structural functionalism, social problems should be resolved by gradual changes or adaptations within the general framework of an existing social order. This perspective fails to ask fundamental questions that might get to the "roots" of a social system, such as: functionally useful to *whom*? Does a segment in society take advantage of the system by exploiting some others? Indeed, the root causes of several social problems exist in the exploitation and oppression of some groups over others. Hence, for better understanding of social problems, in line with social reconstruction, we turn to the next theoretical orientation.

(2) Critical Power-Conflict Perspective

In contrast to functionalism, the conflict theory focuses on social conflicts and opposition rather than on social balance. It is based on the premise that conflict and coercion are not only endemic to existing social structures, but are also the key explanatory concepts to understand how societies with social problems operate. The basis for conflict is structured social inequality and injustice stemming from power and control vested in a privileged elite. One specific conflict perspective, called *Marxist analysis*, studies economic inequality, while a second one called *critical theory* focuses on inequality with respect to authority relationships (in family, workplace, and other areas where obedience to authority is normally demanded). There are contradictions inherent in social organization and they act as agents of change. Once people are aware of contradictions, they work for social transformation.

Many of the ideas of conflict perspective can be traced to the social theories developed by Karl Marx (1818-1883) in the 19th century. Later, Ralf Dahrendorf in Germany and C. Wright Mills in America made significant contributions in the examination of the role of power in society.

Recently critical theory has emerged as a separate perspective from conflict orientation. Critical theorists see their beginnings in the Frankfurt school of thought in Germany and the contributions of Theodore Adorne, Herbert Marcuse, Erich Fromm, and others. Those scholars have been followed by Antonio Gramisci and Jurgen Habermas. Today, critical pedagogy is debated in education based upon the contributions of Freire, an educator in Brazil. He argues that when people become literate, they recognize the oppression in society and develop a new awareness, and the result is social transformation. Other leading critical theorists today are Michael Apple and Henry Giroux, both of whom have published numerous books on education, exploring many questions in critical perspective.

Educational Reconstructionists seem to be in general agreement with critical power-conflict theory. Brameld and others have urged people to take a stand on issues, including controversial ones. In such a situation, conflict is unavoidable. Indeed, conflict is accepted as part of living and people are engaged in a constant struggle to resolve conflicts. One of Brameld's original ideas of was "defensible partiality," which implies that we take sides on controversial issues so long as our positions are defensible.

Remember, reconstructionists see our modern culture in crisis, recognizing all of its problems as well as its prospects. The crisis culture needs a transformation involving fundamental or radical change. Institutions or structures must be modified if our major problems are to be solved. Critical theorists can learn from reconstructionism about the place of a global outlook because problems we face today transcend national boundaries. Critical theory will be stronger if it includes a global outlook while studying and solving problems.

(3) Symbolic Interaction Perspective

Instead of studying large social structures and institutions, the symbolic interaction approach concentrates on the day-to-day communication that occurs when people interact in face-to-face situation. People interact mainly through symbols, and hence the meanings given to words and shared within a culture form the focus of this theory. The process by which meanings come to be learned and shared within the context of a specific culture is the process of socialization. The family is the unit in which people receive their first and most intensive socializing experience. Socialization occurs when a youngster takes roles and learns the appropriate behavior.

George Herbert Mead (1863-1931) with his explanations of social role and generalized other and Charles H. Cooley (1846-1929) with his idea of the "looking glass self" are among the earliest contributors, followed by W. I. Thomas (1863-1947) who coined the phrase "definition of the situation." Recently Peter Berger and Thomas Luckmann, through the notion of "social construction of reality," present society as both "objective reality" *and* "subjective reality." Other contemporary interactionists include Erving Goffman and Herbert Blumer. To them, a fact has no meaning: "Meanings are given to facts and to human actions by human beings."

Educational Reconstruction gains from the notions of interaction and communication advocated by this symbolic interaction perspective. These notions are needed for the creation of democracy and for the people participation that Reconstructionism requires. However, there is a major difference between the two in the scope of the interaction. Reconstructionists see democracy in global terms, while symbolic interaction explains it only in face-to-face situations. But these are not necessarily opposing ideas, because the local and the global orientations can benefit from each other. As noted before, we increasingly realize the global dimensions of social problems whose solutions lie in the cooperation of peoples everywhere on the planet. Today we find peace efforts by many nations around the world to stop war in a specific area of the globe or country. To solve the drug problem in New York City, the cooperation of Colombia in South America has become essential. International cooperation is sought more and more in solving many problems that occur in several different and specific parts of the world, including Bosnia.

Summary and Conclusion

An effective starting point in my teaching of philosophy of education is to examine the social problems and issues of our times. This approach has its philosophical basis in Educational Reconstruction, which I have discussed here by selecting two leaders, both known to me at the personal level: Morris Mitchell, director of Putney Graduate School when I studied there in 1963-64; and Theodore Brameld, my major adviser during doctoral studies at Boston University (1964-67). My association with these two great teachers enabled me to develop the philosophy of Educational Reconstruction which I follow in my teaching. Hence, I not only follow the issues approach in my teaching, but also keep strongly to a specific view in dealing with these issues. This view includes the attempt to transform social structures, maintain a global outlook, and encourage an action orientation. As the scientific studies of social problems are undertaken by sociologists, my classes have benefitted by keeping abreast of developments in this field, as well as in the related field of anthropology.

I emphasize and study three theoretical perspectives followed by sociologists: (1) Structural-Functionalism; (2) Critical Power-Conflict Perspective; and (3) Symbolic Interaction Perspective. Among them, the second—the Critical Power-Conflict Perspective—seems to be in agreement with the Reconstructionist philosophy of education. The common concerns of both Reconstructionism and conflict perspective include an explanation of society with reference to power exercised by dominant and marginal groups as well as the need for and possibility of social transformation.

References

Brameld, T. (1971). *Patterns of Educational Philosophy: Divergence and Convergence in Culturesological Perspective.* New York: Holt, Rinehart & Winston.

Feagin, J. (1986). *Social Problems: A Critical Power-Conflict Perspective.* Englewood Cliffs, NJ: Prentice-Hall.

Freire, P. & D. Macedo. (1987). *Literacy: Reading the Word and the World.* New York: Bergin & Garvey.

Neville, R. (1995). *Normative Cultures.* Albany, NY: State University of New York Press.

Nisbet, R. & R. Merton. (1971). *Contemporary Social Problems.* New York: Harcourt, Brace, Javanovich.

Postman, N. (1995). *The End of Education: Redefining the Values of School.* New York: Alfred A. Knopf.

Stein, P. *et. al.* (1977). *The Family: Functions, Conflicts, and Symbols.* New York: Addison-Wesley.

Thomas, T. (1970). *Indian Educational Reforms in Cultural Perspective.* Delhi, India: S. Chand & Co.

Chapter 3

SOME BASIC TENETS OF EDUCATIONAL RECONSTRUCTION

By Darrol Bussler

Introduction

Theodore Brameld (1970) described the philosophy of Educational Reconstruction as one "infused with commitment to magnetic ideals" (p. 199), while I.B. Berkson (1958) wrote that the democratic principles upon which reconstruction philosophy rests "must have certain credos to affirm" (p. 74). Similarly, Boyd H. Bode (1933) in *The Educational Frontier* suggested that "a democratic procedure ...involves a definite creed or point of view" (p. 27).

What are the "magnetic ideals" of Educational Reconstruction? What is its credo? That is the subject of this chapter, where some of the tenets of Educational Reconstruction philosophy will be identified along with implications for teaching.

Holism:

Context for Tenets of Educational Reconstruction

Twentieth century utopian writer Lewis Mumford in *The Transformation of Man* (1956) criticized previous attempts at developing a new philosophy by stating that earlier philosophies had been too rigid, too self-oriented, and not open to the thought of other views. Although he began by negating an attempt to create another system, Mumford underscored the problem of contemporary philosophers who did not work toward synthesis and unity. Mumford was led to conclude: "To effect a new transformation of [humanity], we must be informed by a philosophy capable of uniting every aspect of human experience, and directing human development through every phase" (p. 232). For the reconstructionist, the unity and transformation of which Mumford wrote is the challenge—transformation of education, transformation of self, and transformation of society. This transformation seeks to create an overall unity.

Present discussion suggests that Educational Reconstruction be considered a response to the need for a new philosophy as expressed by Mumford: "Many attempts to formulate such a philosophy during the last two centuries have been handicapped by the traditional tendency of philosophy itself to create a single watertight system, too confidently complete to admit repair or enlargement by other minds" (p. 231). Brameld's views of reconstruction and its relationship to previous philosophic thought suggest that reconstruction's "borrowing" from other philosophies has served as a means of avoiding a "single watertight system" and as a way of remaining open to "repair and enlargement by other minds." Brameld defined *borrowing* as eclecticism, and it is suggested that eclecticism forms the basis for reconstruction's holistic nature which recognizes that the reconstructionist position is part of a whole, and that the "borrowings," the eclecticism, remind us of the relationship to the whole.

Brameld spent considerable time discussing the relationship of reconstruction to other philosophies, specifically progressive, essential, and perennial perspectives, and discussed the need for eclecticism in philosophy. The discussion examines the essence and relationship of these four philosophic positions.

Brameld (*Power*, 1965) stressed the importance of understanding the relationship between reconstruction and alternative philosophies:

> If we define philosophy as the attempt of any culture to give meaning to itself, and so to its ethos, then reconstructionism must in many ways be built upon the rich thinking and experience of other philosophies of life and education. Reconstructionism borrows much from other philosophies, and makes no pretense to the contrary. (p. 33)

Brameld used two illustrations to help explain the relationship of reconstruction to the other philosophies in his framework. The first illustration was used in *Philosophies of Education in Cultural Perspective* (p. 77). Here one can see that the four philosophies are paired: essentialism and perennialism appear to have much in common while progressivism and reconstructionism share assumptions and conclusions.

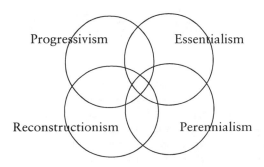

Brameld insisted that

each position has something in common with the others.... A diagram may help here if we bear in mind that it does not intend to measure the precise *extent* of overlappings either among the four positions regarded as wholes, or among individual advocates of these positions, who may differ in the degree to which they accept one or another of the several points of view. (p. 76)

A limitation of a graphic representation such as this one is its failure to identify commonalties and differences. Brameld recognized the limitation: "It does not intend to measure the precise extent of overlappings." Brameld's use of the visual served as a means to underscore his holistic view of the interdependence of the positions within philosophic thought.

A decade later Brameld (*Power,* 1965) used an illustration to show the relationship of the four philosophies as a continuum:

I want to convey through the broken lines of the diagram that the four philosophies are not sharply separable. The four are not to be regarded as distinct categories which have no relation with each other. A continuum suggests that each flows into the other, and that there is some relation among all. (p. 29)

Brameld indicated that the four philosophies presented four socio-political positions: reconstruction the radical, progressive the liberal, essential the conservative, and perennial the regressive. In political terms, Brameld held educational reconstruction to be on the far left and the perennial perspective as the far right.

With this illustration, Brameld explained that the essential and perennial perspectives represent views which emphasize the transmission of culture, while progressive and reconstructionist emphasize innovation in the survival and evolvement of culture.

In very general terms, Brameld perceived the following primary contributions by the other three philosophies upon which educational reconstruction builds:

• **perennial:** the value of purpose; action must move toward a decided-upon direction; it is of little value if it is action without direction.

• **essential:** the need for education to be transmissive. The continuation of culture can only be accomplished if it is transmitted.

• **progressive:** change through action. (pp. 33-34)

The differentiation between progressive and reconstructionist philosophies is sometimes difficult to comprehend; Brameld was the first to admit it. In his first major work (*Patterns,* 1950), Brameld explained that "in certain ways, the two theories are so similar that one may properly raise the question as to whether they deserve to be separately classified" (p. 390). In spite of similarities between the progressive and reconstructionist positions, Brameld was consistent in explaining their difference. The following is an example:

First, progressivism...has remained too largely a philosophy of means, of methods, of processes...the emphasis...is on "how" more often then on "what," on process more often than product, on means more often than on ends...

The second lack is that progressivism in broadest perspective remains an anthropocentric philosophy. That is, it too easily sloughs off the fact that [humanity] is, after all, but a minute segment of the universe.

Or may I put it differently? Progressivism is too often relatively indifferent to the mystery of existence, and hence to the ultimate mystery both of the human being and of the cosmos itself. Again I recognize that the great philosophers of pragmatism and progressivism by no means ignore these concerns. But their focus of attention is not on the existential dimension of [humanity] and nature; it is rather on the scientific, practical processes by which [humanity] understands and controls [humanity] and nature. The emphasis is rationalistic, the emphasis is instrumental, the emphasis is on intelligent direction of [humanity] and nature. Progressivism is not greatly troubled with the mysterious yet immediate existences that precede [humanity] and follow [humanity]. (*Power*, pp. 81-82)

In Brameld's explanation of the close relationship between the two philosophies in the preceding paragraphs, it may be noted that the holistic nature of reconstruction is evident. In short, reconstruction considers "how and what," "process and product," "means and ends," "the rational and the mysterious." Howard Ozman in *Educational Reconstruction: Promise and Challenge* (1973) summarized: "Basically, reconstructionists would like to link thought with action, theory with practice, and intellect with activism" (p. 144).

The subject of holism or eclecticism in Educational Reconstruction also relates to analytic philosophy and critical pedagogy, the latter to be discussed at the end of this chapter. Analytic philosophy, or more accurately the analytic movement, is not a systematic philosophy as those identified in the preceding discussion. Analytic philosophers oppose categorizing ideas into philosophical systems, preferring to note the overlapping of ideas. A unifying theme among the analytic philosophers is clarification of language, concepts, and methods—language analysis and meaning. Analytic philosophers such as Wittgenstein stress the importance of looking for meaning in context rather than accepting meaning from another time, place, or philosophic category.

Reconstructionists are open to the idea of analytic clarification. According to Frank A. Stone (1996), formerly at the University of

Connecticut and a member of the Society for Educational Reconstruction (SER),

> From our point of view, the beauty of reconstruction is that it is, as the current saying in our church goes, "open and affirming." We have no difficulty seeing and applying the analytic methods, where they are appropriate, while insisting that education is much more inclusive than the rational articulation of theory.

Stone goes on to clarify how reconstruction and analytic philosophers differ. "They [analytics] simply seem to miss the imagination, creativity, and metaphor that is so vital to good teaching/learning." Thus, reconstructionists accept part of analytic thought and, like the analytic philosophers, look beyond the boundaries separating individual philosophic systems.

The holistic perception of reconstructionists—looking beyond boundaries and seeing overlappings—is grounded in their view of culture; Educational Reconstruction is a culture-based philosophy. Therefore, culture is the first tenet presented for discussion.

Culture

Culture is viewed as the basis for human development and as an all-encompassing tenet in this discussion which provides the framework for reconstructionist thought and action. William Boyer made the point in his introduction to Brameld and Midori Matsuyama's *Tourism and Cultural Learning* (1978): "Everyone is transformed *by* and is also a transformer *of* culture" (p. v).

The importance of culture for Educational Reconstruction is a logical extension of the turn-of-the-century shift from education's focus on the individual to a focus on the individual within a social context. A description of that shift is provided by John Dewey and John L. Childs in *The Educational Frontier*. It may be important to note that this description was written in 1933, providing the advantage of retrospection:

> [The new] Education was presented as a process of transmission and reconstruction of culture; the dependence of the individual upon the resources, material and spiritual, of the collective heritage was stressed. The need for enabling individuals to take part in the task of a constantly changing society was put in the foreground of

educational philosophy. The idea that the school should be itself a form of community life, and that this principle should be applied in discipline, instruction, and the conduct of recitation, gained appreciable though far from universal recognition.

This change in the underlying concepts of education gave promise of a type of educational philosophy which would have closer contact with the realities of present day life than was possessed by the older theory. It contained within itself the seed of efforts to bring about a definite integration of activities within the school with the activities going on in the larger community beyond the school walls. (pp. 32-33)

The importance of the relationship of the individual and the social is expressed concisely in a pre-turn-of-the-century statement by Dewey (1959; Cremin, ed.): "Society is an organic union of individuals" (p. 22). Dewey's interest in the social is evident in the title of his book *School and Society* published as the new century began. Dewey concluded that passivity and listening must give way to a process where truth is defined by the collective experience of society. The shift from pure individualism, to individualism within a social context was articulated in *My Pedagogic Creed* (1897):

I believe that this conception [adjustment of individual activity on the basis of social consciousness] has due regard for both the individualistic and socialistic ideals. It is duly individual because it recognizes the formulation of a certain character as the only genuine basis of right living. It is socialistic because it recognizes that this right character is not to be formed by merely individual precept, example, or exhortation, but rather by the influence of a certain form of institutional or community life upon the individual, and that the social organism through the school, as its organ, may determine ethical results. (Cremin, p. 30)

The turn of the century saw the shift from a gradual development of individualism, to an individualism within a social context. Dewey and other first-generation reconstructionists articulated this change which, for reconstructionists, is a basic one and serves as a prelude for viewing culture as "the all-encompassing whole" and recognizing that education relates to it directly and influentially.

The ultimate goal for reconstructionists is greater social control over culture. Brameld (*Ends,* 1950) called for a "control of the industrial system, of public services, and of cultural and natural resources by and for the common people" (p. 17). This control over culture can be gained through a system of thought which moves to action; the system of thought is reconstruction. As previously cited by Ozman: "Reconstructionism is a culture-centered philosophy" (p. 150).

The framework for a workable view of culture was provided by Edward B. Tyler, to whom Brameld called attention in his discussions of culture. Tyler defined culture as "that complex whole which includes knowledge, belief, art, moral, law, custom, and any other capabilities and habits acquired by [humanity as members] of society." It seems important to note that in Tyler's definition, the reference to *whole* is in accord with the reconstructionist's holistic view. Also important for reconstructionists is Tyler's reference to *acquire*, indicating that culture is not a part of the gene pool. For example, animals have societies which are developed through instinct, while humans develop cultures which are transmitted and adapted through learning. A third important concept in Tyler's definition, *society*, emphasizes that humans must live with each other. Culture is not created in isolation.

The groundwork had been laid. The importance of culture was emphasized by George S. Counts in *Dare the School Build a New Social Order?* (1932). Counts underscored the power which culture has on human life: culture is the basis for human development. He explained in a significant passage:

> There is a fallacy that [humans are] born free. As a matter of fact, [humans are] born helpless. [They achieve] freedom, as a race and as an individual, through the medium of culture. The most crucial of all circumstances conditioning human life is birth into a particular culture. By birth one becomes a Chinese, an Englishman, A Hottentot, a Sioux Indian, a Turk, or a one-hundred-percent American. Such a range of possibilities may appear too shocking to contemplate, but it is the price that one must pay in order to be born. Nevertheless even if a given soul should happen by chance to choose a Hottentot for a mother, it should thank its lucky star that it was born into the Hottentot culture rather than entirely free. By being nurtured on a body of culture, however backward and limited it may be comparatively, the individual is at once imposed upon and liberated. The child is terribly imposed upon by being compelled through the accident of birth to learn one language

rather than another, but without some language [humans] would never become [human]. Any language, even the most poverty-stricken, is infinitely better than none at all. In the life cycle of the individual many choices must of necessity be made, and the most fundamental and decisive of these choices will always be made by the group. This is so obvious that it should require no elaboration. (pp. 13-14)

Reconstructionists have held that not only does culture determine the human being, as Counts explained above, but that a philosophy can guide human beings to develop culture, which, in turn, provides guidance. As Kenneth D. Benne (1956) in "The Content of a Contemporary Philosophy of Education" stated:

The responsible determination of the content of a living philosophy of education (and of a living philosophy as well) can be made only through a diagnosis of the culture in terms of its major normative and intellectual conflicts. For these mark the places where fundamental intellectual clarification is most needed and, in the view of history, possible. (pp. 127-130)

If culture is the cause from which ideas come, and for which ideas are developed, how can those ideas actually affect the culture? The answer leads the discussion to a second basic reconstructionist tenet: the belief in education as an agent to both transmit and transform culture.

Action in the classroom: If I realize that my twenty-nine students are twenty-nine different cultures coming into my classroom today, what actions will I carry out to reflect this realization?

Education as Transmission and Transformation

Brameld's visual image (*Power,* p. 15) reveals how recostructionists see the relationship between culture and education. The connection of major areas of culture and the way in which Brameld believed education related to all of them is evident. Brameld pointed out the danger in using this type of image; it could communicate the idea that culture was static:

Actually, no such thing as a static culture can be found anywhere on earth. So I would like to think of our model as moving very rapidly in time from one point to another. Every one of these seven areas...is beset with conflicts. Each one is suffering from tension between forces that tend to stabilize traditional patterns, and forces that tend to move toward more or less drastic modification of those patterns. (p. 15)

In Brameld's visual model, all areas of culture are touched by education; it is the reconstructionist view that education is the chief change agent of culture.

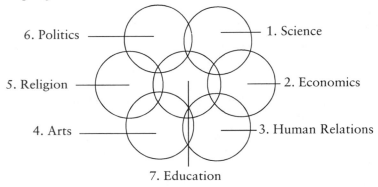

6. Politics   1. Science
5. Religion   2. Economics
4. Arts   3. Human Relations
7. Education

This section will analyze the reconstructionist idea of education as change agent and then explore reconstructionist views on the roles of the school, and indoctrination and objectivity in teaching and learning.

The idea of education as change agent of culture was not a new one for reconstructionists. For example, Immanuel Kant believed that the schools in any society should have the academic freedom to cultivate the perfections of humanity with a new order. In early American development, Thomas Jefferson saw education as the means to improving the condition of human life. For the reconstructionists, education is the central focus; education is the means. It is the source for both the continuation and modification of culture. In short, education is at the heart of reconstruction philosophy.

Dewey provided the twentieth-century base for the reconstructionists' emphasis upon education. At the beginning of his writing career, Dewey took a firm position regarding education's role. In *My*

Pedagogic Creed, Dewey had gone on record: "I believe that education is the fundamental method of social progress and reform" (Cremin, p. 30). Dewey's colleague, Childs (1959), noted Dewey's view of education playing both roles of transmission and transformation:

> Education for John Dewey, was neither a luxury nor a mere adornment; it was rather a life necessity. It is through education, he perceived, that each child achieves...distinctively human attributes, and it is also through education that a society perpetuates and deliberately modifies its way of living. (p. 128)

Childs' use of the terms *perpetuates* and *modifies* indicates this view of a twofold role for education: transmission and transformation.

A major emphasis was upon education's modification, change, transformation, and reconstruction of society. In *The Quest for Certainty*, Dewey stated that education "holds the key to orderly social reconstruction" (p. 252). It is this view which extended Educational Reconstruction beyond previous philosophic views such as the essential and perennial, becoming the primary reason why education's transformative role would be viewed as the heart of Educational Reconstruction.

Other progressive educators followed Dewey's emphasis on education's role of reconstruction. Boyd H. Bode (1927) wrote: "The school becomes an agency maintained by society for its own progressive reconstruction" (p. 262). Harold Rugg (1931) asserted: "Now the school is the only organized agency at all competent to cope with the problem of developing in our youth an understanding of this complicated order" (p. vii). The concept received its greatest attention, however, in Counts' *Dare the School Build a New Social Order?* Counts gave the challenge to make "education as a force for social regeneration" (pp. 30-31). He saw this regeneration as action, as building rather than mere contemplation of culture, its past and present:

> Our Progressive schools therefore cannot rest content with giving children an opportunity to study contemporary society in all of its aspects. This of course must be done, but I am convinced that they should go farther. If the schools are to be really effective, they must become centers for the building, and not merely contemplation, of our civilization. This does not mean that we should endeavor to

promote particular reforms through the educational system. We should, however, give to our children a vision of the possibilities which lie ahead and endeavor to enlist their loyalties and enthusiasms in the realization of the vision. Also our social institutions and practices, all of them, should be critically examined in the light of such a vision. (p. 37)

A later example of the school as instrument of social change was mentioned in the first chapter of this publication with a reference to the Citizenship Schools initiated by Septima Clark and Myles Horton. Also mentioned was William O. Stanley's idea that education is more than giving out information; education shapes and molds.

There are several terms which reconstructionists use to describe this dual role. Berkson (1958) referred to the double responsibility as "one of *conservation* and one of *reconstruction*" (emphasis added). To him, conservation was "the heritage of the humanities, the classic literature, and the political, philosophic, and religious ideas which exemplify Western civilization," while reconstruction meant "the bringing of a new democratic world order into being" (pp. 209-210).

Brameld's view is similar to that of Berkson, although Brameld used different terminology. Brameld saw the roles of education as *transmissive* and *transformative*. The first role, transmissive, includes a focus on all that has been and is, in other words past and present, while the transformative role focuses on the future. The latter, transformative, reveals the influence of Mumford through Brameld.

The concept and term *transformation,* as used by Mumford, became common usage for reconstructionists; it often appeared in reconstructionist writing, and it continues to be used by present-day reconstructionists. For example, David R. Conrad, a charter member of the SER, entitled one of his books *Education for Transformation: Implications in Lewis Mumford's Ecohumanism.*[1]

In *Tourism as Cultural Learning,* Brameld and Matsuyama referred to the two roles as "transmissive value orientation" and "transformative value orientation" (pp. 36-37). Brameld (*Power,* 1965) summarized his view in these words:

> Remember, then, that the educative process seen in the anthropological context of organized ways of life is invariably a *bi-polar process* [emphasis added], or, I should better say, a complementary process. On the one hand, it is a process of stabilizing, of transmitting, of guaranteeing continuity to the culture. On the other hand,

it is a process of correcting, improving, and altering the acquired characteristics of past generations. (pp. 12-13)

In addition to Berkson's terms of *conservation* and *reconstruction,* and Brameld's *transmissive* and *transformative,* there are two other terms which add another perspective to the double role of education. Brameld (*Explosive,* 1965) referred to the two roles as *acquire* and *inquire.* The learner may "acquire" culture through education; however, rather than playing a passive role only, that is, "acquiring" from someone else, the learner also "inquires," which has a more active connotation. Through this dynamic inquiring process, the learner may begin to modify the culture.

> According to this second view, humans *acquire* by a process of *inquiring* into the nature of their culture. And inquiring, as John Dewey...implies in such a book as *Freedom and Culture,* is [humanity's] capacity to engage actively and critically in the events of...cultural experience—to take them apart, as it were, and to rearrange them in more satisfying, efficient, workable ways than before. (p. 61)

David C. Woolman, a member of SER, interpreted Brameld's view more specifically. He suggested that Brameld viewed education as having four responsibilities: "These include the restoration of lost cultural values, the preparation of students to adapt to new demands, the transmission of important customs of contemporary culture, and the transformation of culture by teaching students how to recognize and resolve problems of the present society" (p. 219). It appears that the first three roles can be included in the category of transmission: lost cultural values, adaptation, and present customs. It seems that the two broad processes of transmission and transformation adequately explain Brameld's view and that of other reconstructionists.

In summary, reconstructionists such as Berkson, Brameld, and Matsuyama view the role of education as twofold. First, a conserving, transmitting, acquiring role; second, a reconstructing, transforming, and inquiring role. The concepts of transmitting and transforming remain the common language of reconstructionists today. For example, the concept of transformation is prominent in the goals of SER.

Reconstructionists do not merely speak in general terms but become specific about what the transformative role of education should be. A major emphasis was identified by Berkson(1943): "The school has the duty of instilling a consistent conception of democracy and of inducing a thorough application of its principles in life" (pp. 303-304). Some years earlier, Dewey referred to education as "the midwife" of democracy." Dewey's colleague, William H. Kilpatrick, joined in emphasizing the democratic theme by drawing attention to the increasing size of organizations and structures, and the need for the individual to be heard. Specifically, Kilpatrick (1926) held:

> The school must somehow help people to assert themselves, somehow help them to overcome the threats of overpowering bigness. While size of scale may help with production, it threatens danger to the individual. The school must help the individual fight off the danger. (p. 71)

Counts (1938) referred to an early reference concerning the importance of education's role, the writing of an untutored Massachusetts farmer William Manning (1798): "Learning & Knowledge is assential to the preservation of Libberty & unless we have more of it amongue us we Cannot Seporte our Libertyes Long" (p. 178). A more recent view is that of William B. Stanley (1992):

> ...a reconceptualized reconstructionism would aim at the realization of the basic human interest in practical competence and the sociocultural conditions necessary for praxis.... Such praxis involves the simultaneous transmission and transformation of our cultures, while also challenging the value of both processes in a world in which we can never fully grasp the dimensions of otherness. (pp. 221-222)

Reconstructionists see a close relationship between the school and the community. Bruce Raup (1936) perceived the need for cooperation between the school and other agencies in *Education and Organized Interests in America*. Raup held that the function of the school was to participate actively with other agencies in society in order to manage living together. Rugg (1931) joined his Teachers College colleague, calling for a school-centered community: "A society in which home, government, industries, trade, farms, organizations, all the social agencies, will perceive their educational as well as their maintenance functions."[2] It is proposed that the practice of service-learning with the emphasis on service in community has its roots in educational reconstruction philosophy as described by Rugg, who went on to write: "The task of transforming our communities into culture societies, therefore, is essentially the task of making every social agency in the community conscious of its educational possibilities and determined to live up to its obligations" (p. 288).

Rugg and Raup were not alone. H. Gordon Hullfish (1933) saw the responsibility of education beyond that of the school:

> The school, to be sure, is not to be asked to accept sole responsibility for the remaking of society. It has too long been our habit to "pass the buck," as we say, to the school on crucial social issues, and we have come now to realize that at its best the school is but one educative influence in the students whom it touches. (pp. 160-161)

Brameld's view (1950) was consistent with Raup, Rugg, and Hullfish:

> The traditional dualism which has separated school and community should be dissolved. Rather, the community, with all its complex institutions and problems, should itself become a school. (*Ends,* p. 150)

Brameld went on to define this view of "school":

> The good school of today and tomorrow thus extends into the highways and byways of city and country—everywhere that people are living and working. The symbolic walls which surround traditional schools should be torn down, so that there may be a constant stream of two-way traffic between libraries, laboratories, recreation halls of the school proper and the community around them. By "two-way traffic" we mean not only, therefore, that children should spend a much larger proportion of their time participating in the life of the community, under expert guidance, but that adults would regard the school as a neighborhood center to which they come for recreation, companionship, group experiences, and for constant help in solving their local problems.

Brameld's description is similar to, if not identical to, the concept of community education as its is practiced in states such as Minnesota and Michigan. The concept and practice of community education was mentioned in the first chapter with a reference to the work of Morris R. Mitchell. Of particular interest is the idea of community education becoming a means to address community problems. In reconstructionist terms, the school becomes the means to transform the community; the school becomes the catalyst for the process of community development through the democratic process. Educational Reconstruction can be considered a philosophic base for the practice of dynamic community education. For example, community education played the role of catalyst for community development in South St. Paul, Minnesota. The community had been declared an economically depressed area by the federal government. The public school's community education department began a process of uniting city government, the schools, faith communities, business and service communities in efforts toward community revitalization. The efforts were recognized by the League of Cities in 1990 when the city was named an All-America City; the criteria for the award includes involvement of citizens "solving their local problems." The South St. Paul action was based on Educational Reconstruction: the school transforming the community through the democratic process.

One of the principles of community education is lifelong learning, which was of interest to early reconstructionists. It was Kilpatrick who expressed the need for this view in 1932 by saying that "mere school education cannot possibly suffice for the whole of life. To think otherwise is to misconceive and belie the very meaning of education in relation to life. Education goes on as life goes on" (p. 50). Reconstructionists conceive education occurring in many settings beyond formal schools.

Reconstructionists view the value of lifelong education not only in terms of learning new skills and accumulating new information but, more importantly, as a means to maintain an attitude that remains open to the world. Bode (1927) emphasized the point:

> I like to think of education as a process which, if I may put it that way, extends the period of childhood indefinitely. The social pressure, unless it is counteracted in some way, makes us old fogies before our time, robs us of the freshness, the flexibility, the eagerness for new vistas in which the child is so immensely superior to the adult. (p. 261)

While education is viewed as a lifelong process of transforming individuals and society, reconstructionists also believe that schools must transform themselves. This theme is a major point in the *Educational Frontier*, where Hullfish and Thayer (1933) placed an emphasis on the necessity for school reform: "It is reasonable to expect the school to face frankly the fact that it will not contribute to the reconstruction of the social process until it seriously experiments with the reconstruction of its own procedures" (p. 210). In short, reconstructionists believe that while education transforms society, schools must simultaneously be self-transforming. In present-day language, this transforming is referred to as school reform; reconstructionists have been urging school reform from the beginning.

The roles of transmission and transformation raise the question of method. How does education both transmit and transform culture? This question moves the discussion to the role that indoctrination plays in the educational process, a key area of interest for reconstructionists and one in which there was considerable controversy. Kilpatrick's view (1939), however, provides a reconstructionist perspective on indoctrination:

> If, then, we believe in democracy, we shall avoid indoctrination. Democracy, to be itself, cannot indoctrinate even itself. (p. 57)

Kilpatrick believed that a certain degree of indoctrination was inevitable due to the particular environment in which one is raised. Kilpatrick (1940) proposed a conclusion which represents a reconstructionist position:

> The general conclusion is easy. I shall teach the actual habits required in life as the need arises, taking care always that the accompanying attitudes are the best attainable. In connection, I shall teach as much of the "why" as I feasibly can. At the first this "why" part will be exactly nill. Beginning later, the "why" will from then on receive more and more attention. When sufficient growth has been attained (but as early as feasible), the "why" of the previously learned "what" will be brought to the bar of attention. At all times the aim will be the earliest and fullest measure of thinking compatible with other just demands of the situation. In no instance shall we allow any doctrine to be enthroned even approximately beyond recall, especially in the matter of our own cherished beliefs. And we shall avoid as much as we can commitment to doctrines on any authoritarian basis, encouraging early efforts at suspended judgment and often suggesting opposed positions to our own. Our consistent aim shall be not only to avoid "indoctrination" but to build positively against it. (pp. 173-174)

From a reconstructionist view, a danger of indoctrination is offered by T.V. Smith in *The Democratic Way of Life* (1926): Telling someone what to think is the equivalent of telling someone not to think at all.

The issue of indoctrination relates to neutrality and objectivity which became topics of discussion. Should education be neutral? Can education be objective—without emotion or personal prejudice? Reconstructionists believe that it is impossible. Views and biases should openly be presented, and appropriate time and energy ought to be given to presenting opposing views and biases. Counts, in *Education and the Foundations of Human Freedom* (1962), went to some length to show how indoctrination in education had often falsified history, misrepresented institutions and nations, and propagated false doctrines resulting in great detriment to others. Counts concluded: "All human experience demonstrates that education in any living society is never neutral" (p. 53). Ozman (1973) expressed a similar view: "There are no neutral positions; and even if there were, we would be reminded of the contention that 'the hottest spot in hell is reserved for those who in moral times remain neutral'" (p. 143).

To summarize, education is a basic tenet in Educational Reconstruction, given the dual roles of transmitting (maintaining) and transforming (changing) culture. Without this tenet, Educational Reconstruction could not exist as a viable collection of thought. One could be tempted to assert that education is *the* basic tenet. Such an assertion would negate the holistic nature of Educational Reconstruction and the non-absolutist stance which will be discussed under "Values" later in this chapter.

As reconstructionists place emphasis on education as the transforming agent of society, a question emerges. Why does society need to be transformed? Reconstructionist responses are the subject of the next section.

Action in the school system/community: The community has lost 6,000 jobs through down-sizing and lay-offs. What role can our public school system play in community redevelopment?

Action in the classroom: If we are discussing controversial issues such as abortion, gun control, prayer in the schools, what role do I, as a teacher, have in these dialogues?

Action in the classroom: What learning ends (objectives, outcomes) in a subject I'm presently teaching could my

---

students learn through service-learning in a community organization/agency?

Action in the school system/community: If we see our school system as a community school, who will be involved? What educational services will be provided and to whom? What other services could co-locate in the school? How will these be determined? What role will the school play?

Crisis and Speed

According to reconstructionists, education is in a race, and that race is with disaster. Consequently, reconstructionists believe there is a state of crisis. A twentieth century prophet, H.B. Wells, published *The Outline of History* (1920) in which he wrote: "Human history becomes more and more a race between education and catastrophe." According to Counts (1962), this statement was quoted more frequently at educational gatherings in this country than any other (p. 48).

The idea of a crisis culture had been given prominence by the events of the Great Depression in the 1930s. According to Berkson (1940), the sense of crisis was prompted by the fact that the Depression was "the first crisis in history not confined to a few countries or to one continent, but embracing the four corners of the earth" (p. 206).

From the crisis of the Depression in the thirties, the world went immediately into another, the Second World War. Then came the Korean conflict, Sputnik, the Cuban crisis, Vietnam, and the treat of nuclear war. In the later decades of the twentieth century, other crises gained attention, such as poverty, over-population, and a variety of oppressions such as racism. In retrospect, each decade seemed to add a sense of a new or even greater crisis to that which the previous decade had already established. Reconstructionists view the world as being in crisis.

Brameld (*Toward,* 1956) consistently referred to this state of crisis:

> The second half of our century may well be the most crucial period that humanity has faced since the dawn of history. [Humanity] has finally attained the capacity to destroy [its] own species. We have no other choice than to prevent, if we can, this horrible consequence of our scientific genius. Nor have we time to lose. (p. vii)

Brameld not only referred to the condition of crisis but also emphasized the importance of rapidly addressing it, another common theme in reconstructionist thought.

Reconstructionists believe quick action becomes of the utmost importance. Reconstructionists such as Brameld share the conviction that urgency is needed. This idea pushed early reconstructionists beyond progressivism which, they argued, was too slow and too weak in purpose.

But what is meant by crisis? Brameld defined it(*Power,* 1965):

> ...a major dislocation—a dislocation of the fundamental institutions, habits, practices, attitudes of any given culture or any section of a culture. When a point is reached in which the major functions, the major structures, the major purposes of a culture or subculture are thrown out of joint, then its member often find themselves bewildered, lost, uprooted. They and their culture are in a state of crisis. A turning point in their history has been reached. (pp. 10-11)

With the conclusion of the Cold War, one might conclude that the chief crisis to which reconstructionists have been referring for the past fifty years has ended. That is not true from the reconstructionist view. Reconstructionist writers in *Global Images of Peace and Education* (1987) focus on such issues as the ethics of nuclear deterrence, economic injustice and work alienation, genocide prevention, and global hunger. Other reconstructionists focus on issues such as economic revitalization, ecology, greater equity of resources, and the needs of women and children. Reconstructionists view other situations as gravely as war and with no less concern than those of previous decades.

Brameld wrote a description of American culture which may still hold true (*Toward,* 1956): "Our culture can be said to be suffering from 'schizoid' tendencies—that is, tendencies toward splitting and division so acute as to prevent mutual understanding or reconciliation between those who hold opposing attitudes or advocate opposing courses of action" (p. 47). In *The Teacher as World Citizen*, Brameld argued there was yet another crisis, that of complacency which was a result of comfort which is "measured by how many objects of 'conspicuous consumption'...that you or I are able to parade before our peers in order to prove that we 'have made it'" (pp. 35-36). This comfort, according to Brameld (*Power,* 1965), lulled the American culture into a belief that no crisis existed:

> Large numbers of American citizens would be chagrined to be told
> that they are living in the midst of crisis. Never defeated in a world
> war, we Americans tend to be complacent and to think that, after
> all, we are pretty secure, if not even invincible. Perhaps I should use
> a stronger word than complacent; we are—smug. (p. 14)

The American culture could, according to Brameld (1955), no longer
afford to live in this state of complacency since "oceans are too
narrow, flight too swift, weapons too destructive" (p. 386).

To summarize, reconstructionists believe that a global crises
exists and that speed in responding to it is vital. Ozman (1973)
expressed this view when he wrote of reconstructionists: "[They] feel
that we cannot wait for the kinds of gradual reform advocated by
most philosophies, due particularly to the fact that our very survival
may depend on the kinds of immediate steps that need to be taken now
to make society more humanistic and productive" (p. 141).

Reconstructionists' belief that society is in a state of crisis may
lead one to believe that they have a negative, pessimistic perspective.
In actuality, reconstructionists are as positive as they appear to sound
negative. While Educational Reconstruction may be called a philosophy of crisis, it may also be termed a philosophy of hope. As Brameld
stated in *Education as Power:* "A crisis is always characterized by
both danger and promise" (p. 20). Again, the holistic nature of reconstruction becomes apparent.

Action in the classroom: What crises exist in our school or
community and what can students and I do to become
involved while learning content of subject curricula?

Hope

It is not unusual to find reconstructionists who write or speak of
crisis and hope together. Counts (1932) exemplified the characteristic
of seeing crisis and hope simultaneously in *Dare the School Build a
New Social Order?*

> One can only imagine what Jeremiah would say if he could step out
> of the pages of the Old Testament and cast his eyes over this vast
> spectacle so full of tragedy and of menace.
>
> The point should be emphasized, however, that the present situation

is also freighted with hope and promise. The age is pregnant with possibilities. There lies within our grasp the most humane, the most beautiful, the most majestic civilization ever fashioned by any people. (p. 35)

Nearly thirty years later, Brameld wrote in a similar vein in "Imperatives for a Reconstructed Philosophy of Education" in *School and Society* (1959), where he presented two premises: the first, that the world was in the greatest period of crisis in human history; the second, that "[humankind] is now approaching the opportunity to achieve a world civilization of abundance, health, and humane capacity that is as life-affirming and promising as the crisis symbolized by sputniks and hydrogen bombs is life-denying and dreadful" (p. 18).

Just a year earlier, Berkson (1958) had written in a like vein:

We are entering a new stage in world civilization—a stage continuous with the previous liberalist era but which differs from it in a number of essentials. There is no final knowing of what [humanity] will do with [its] many inventions—but there is hope as well as the possibility of doom. (p. 102)

The essence of hope is characteristic of reconstructionists. Ozman (1973) described reconstructionists as "optimistic people" (p. 146). Hope appears to be basic to reconstructionists; some would argue that one cannot be considered a reconstructionist without having hope. For example, Conrad's view of reconstructionists (1987) as hopeful people is evident when he discusses Ivan Illich, whom he contends is not a reconstructionist:

His [Illich] whole notion of deschooling sets him apart from reconstructionists, who have hope. Illich has no hope for public education. Reconstructionist philosophy is hopeful; it builds upon rather than destroys. Reconstructionists have not lost faith.

In Conrad's statement one not only sees the emphasis on the concept of hope, but also notes the reconstructionist position which builds upon that which exists. Conrad's statement supports the reconstructionist idea of eclecticism discussed earlier. Rather than destroying or totally ignoring earlier philosophies, educational reconstruction builds on previous ideas.

The characteristic of building upon that which has previously existed rather than destroying, suggests a non-violent approach. It includes not only the world of ideas and institutions, but the physical world as well, indicated in the following section.

> **Action in the classroom:** Students and I identify and study problems and crises, which, in the end, caused positive changes and results.

Non-Violence

A reconstructionist approach to bring about change is based on ideas shared through a systematic process of persuasion; reconstructionists do not hold with the use of physical force to make change; Educational Reconstruction is a process of change through non-violence.

Stone (1987) brings the tenet of non-violence to the fore. He believes democratic decision-making is a major process in Educational Reconstruction practice and contends that

> This relates to the idea of non-violent confrontation. Certainly there will be disagreement; that's basic. However, it's educating people to disagree through non-violent methods.

Stone's reference to the Citizenship Schools in the first chapter is an example of a non-violent approach to change; students in the schools learned how to discuss common problems and to resolve issues without violence.

The reconstructionist's position on non-violence can be understood through the views of Brameld presented earlier in this chapter. Brameld (*Patterns,* 1950) believed there must be a consistent practice of what he termed "maximum sensitivity and penetrating criticism" (p. 525). For reconstructionists, there is always the desire to reach the optimum possible solution, conclusion, or in the best possible outcome, an agreement. Reaching that agreement may mean a great deal of disagreement including discussion, debate, or what Stone calls "non-violent confrontation." Brameld stated that this process must always be critical, meaning evaluative, and that it may be necessary for it to include "penetrating criticism."

Within this process of penetrating criticism, there is a respect for the views of others and for those who represent those views, regardless of how disagreeable the views or how disagreeable the person or persons who represent those views. There is the supreme respect for the right to state one's view without fear. Within that process of penetrating criticism there is always the value of "maximum sensitivity."

The two notions of criticism and sensitivity may, at times, seem incompatible. Yet, the tenet of non-violence is basic to democracy upon which reconstructionists base the entire process of decision-making and implementation. Without a commitment to non-violence, democracy, as defined by Educational Reconstruction, cannot function.

> **Action in the classroom:** What process are we implementing in our classroom and in our school to practice non-violence in solving differences?

Democracy

The theory and practice of democracy is at the heart of Educational Reconstruction. Although any discussion on democracy could touch a variety of aspects, the intent here is: (1) To indicate the importance of democracy from the reconstructionist viewpoint; and (2) To explain Brameld's ideas regarding the roles of the majority and minority, which if practiced, carry out the ideals of democracy as reconstructionists define them. One view of the reconstructionist ideals is expressed by SER through its emphasis on "cooperative power."

As mentioned in the introduction, *The Educational Frontier* (1933) is considered the first major publication to collectively present a reconstructionist position. In it Dewey and Childs made this assertion regarding democracy:

> Upon one thing we take our stand. We frankly accept the democratic tradition in its moral and human import. That is our premise and we are concerned to find out and state its implications for present life under present conditions, in order that we may know what it entails for theory and practice of public education. (p. 72)

The acceptance of the democratic tradition was not new, for other writers within and outside education had already expressed the idea. For example, I.L. Kandel in *Essays in Comparative Education* (1930) wrote that the first American ideal is democracy. T.V. Smith advanced his ideas on the ideals of democracy in 1926, followed by later printings with his colleague Eduard C. Lindeman in which they concluded their work with seven propositions, the final one relating to democracy and education: "The modern democratic way of life can be realized in this age of self-consciousness only if its precepts and way of living are incorporated in the educational system" (p. 148).

Berkson (1940) offered a complementary notion to Dewey and Childs' slogan, "On Democracy we take our stand": "To make a true philosophy of life out of this slogan, it must be more completely elaborated; its meaning must be expounded again and again; its applications to current issues must be made clear in great detail" (p. 53). Berkson expanded his ideas on democracy by focusing on the social nature of philosophy, including both the ethical and the political. For Berkson and reconstructionists in general, the ethical was based on the belief "in the inestimable worth of each individual person" (p. 60).

The emphasis on democracy continued with Brameld, for whom democracy was at the core of Educational Reconstruction, affecting every other belief and action. The reason was simple. According to Brameld (*Emerging,* 1965), democracy produced positive results as no other kind of government: "Democracy, more than any form of society devised thus far by [humanity], is capable of providing greatest happiness for the largest number of people on the earth" (p. 223). One can begin to see how Brameld would view the relationship of democracy and the world.

Brameld wrote of the democratic process in simple terms (1955), emphasizing power, or more correctly, authority: "the belief that the majority of people in any organized society should be the sole sovereign *authority* [emphasis added] over the whole of society; conversely, no single individual or minority group should hold sovereign *authority* [emphasis added] in any organized society" (p. 366). In this quotation, Brameld adds another important component to his view of democracy and the discussion continues to the second point in this section on the majority and minority functions. In *Education for the Emerging Age*, Brameld's definition of democracy pointed to these roles: "The democratic process [is] defined as majority agreement tempered by the privilege of minority opposition" (p. 35). This relationship of distinctly different but complimentary roles is a primary belief of Brameld for it is *the* basis for some of his concepts to be discussed later in this chapter.

Brameld discussed the value and nature of both roles—the

majority and the minority, although he spent more time on the role of the minority. In discussing the role of the majority, Brameld (1955) explained the place of authority: "The majority of people in any organized society should be the sole sovereign authority over the whole of society" (p. 366). Brameld's words reflected an old tradition of democracy explained by Berkson (1940)—the reference to "sovereignty":

> The term democracy is still applied mainly to political affairs, and is dominated by implications arising out of the basic principle of popular sovereignty. This is particularly true as regards British writers, among whom an even narrower usage is observable, that is, a limitation to methods of government. Lord Bryce, a high authority, has it that the essence of democracy is "rule of the majority." In America, too, we have our conservatives who treat with certain aristocratic superciliousness any attempt to broaden the meaning of democracy by giving to it the wider significance of a social program and a humane ideal. (p. 57)

The broadening of which Berkson wrote relates to Brameld's emphasis upon the role of the minority. As noted earlier, Brameld spent more time discussing the role of the minority, perhaps believing that the role of the majority was already well understood through such concepts such as "majority rule," or "whomsoever gets the most votes wins—and has authority." Brameld's view (*Power*, 1965) stressed the opposing, dissenting, challenging role of the minority: "The minority of citizens have the unrestricted privilege of criticizing openly and seeking to persuade the majority at any time that one or another adopted policy requires modification and possibly repudiation" (p. 139). Brameld's reference (*Patterns*, 1950) to the "unrestricted privilege of criticizing openly" may be perceived as a challenge when he wrote: "It should always be part of our responsibility to serve as critic and corrector of those who *have* [emphasis his] agreed" (p. 459). From Brameld's perspective, it was particularly important for the minority to practice that responsibility.

The underlying belief for Brameld's emphasis upon the role of the minority was, at least in part, based on John Stuart Mill's position which, according to Brameld, held that "there must always be a place for minorities so long as it remains unproved that the majority is infallible" (p. 487). Brameld insisted that the "process requires continuous checking of evidence and introduction of fresh evidence;

continuous experimental testing of all important facts and proposals; and continuous public testimony among as many groups as possible—whether dissenting or consenting groups" (p. 370).

The roles of the minority and the majority are the challenges presented by Brameld (*Power,* 1965), which he believed that when practiced, moved human society to adulthood: "The achievement of democracy means that the human race has finally grown up enough to take complete charge of its own affairs" (p. 139). Brameld proposed that Educational Reconstruction be the philosophy that could move the human race from the adolescence of progressivism to the maturity of Educational Reconstruction.

The emphasis upon the tenet of democracy continues in present times. SER lists one of the four central concepts which shape its goals as "social democracy." The Society contends that educational and social policy decisions ought to be democratically made. Schools, SER suggests, should be cooperative communities of learners. The original purpose statement of SER (1968) reflects Educational Reconstruction's emphasis on democracy; the statement identifies "two basic objectives"—the first is "democratic control over the decisions that influence human lives." SER reflects the emphasis upon social justice as a part of the reconstructionist view of democracy.

The application to the classroom is offered by SER Chair Darrol Bussler in "The Democratic Class" (1994) in which he proposes a new model for classroom management. In this model, Bussler begins with the essentialist position which is a "teacher-centered classroom." He then moves the model to the progressivist position of the Progressive Education Movement's "student-centered classroom." Finally, as an Educational Reconstructionist, Bussler combines both the essentialist and progressivist positions into what he terms the "teacher-with-students centered classroom." He cautions that *both* teacher and students are a part of the model. In his work, he finds that teachers who want to move toward the direction of a democratic classroom often give their power (authority) away, allowing students to do whatever they want; when doing that, Bussler contends, the teachers have moved back to the student-centered classroom. He emphasizes that *both* teacher and students have the authority to influence decisions. Bussler defines the democratic classroom as one where the "teachers and students, *together,* make decisions which affect them."

Teacher-Centered Essentialist	Child-Centered Progressive Education Movement	Teacher-with-Students-Centered Reconstructionist: Social Democracy

A summary for this discussion on democracy is an excerpt selected from Ozman's "A Philosophical Perspective." Ozman discusses what he considers to be the basic ideas of reconstruction and includes a list of five sub-captions, one being "Reconstructionism is Democratic."

> Reconstructionism is democratic in the best sense of the term. Reconstructionists feel that people should have control over their lives, and that governments and institutions are only artificial constructs which should serve the interests of people. Reconstructionists do not support any particular ideology for they are aware of the need to change ideologies in ways to make them better. They do insist, however, that whatever changes occur should take place in democratic fashion, with the need for education as a way of making people aware of both problems and possible solutions. Reconstructionists are opposed to authoritarianism and autocracy in every form and help to support the right of people everywhere to govern themselves. (p. 151)

The latter idea of Ozman—people everywhere governing themselves, continues the discussion to include the idea of world community and world government. It is a concept of world-wide interdependence, of humankind as a great family, of the truly great society. The latter was a political phrase made popular during the presidency of Lyndon Johnson; it referred then only to the United States. Reconstructionists' view of a great family and a great society is in broader terms: worldwide.

Action in the classroom: As we put the reconstructionist "teacher-with-students centered classroom" into practice, which components of a Developing Democratic Classroom do we implement: (1) establish classroom *rules;* (2) determine *consequences* for breaking rules; (3) decide *what* to teach/learn; (4) understand *why* we're learning what we're learning; (5) determine *how* to teach/learn; (6) *evaluate* and *celebrate* teaching and learning. (Bussler, p. 43)

76

World Community/World Government

The interest in world community is, of course, not new with the twentieth century. Marcus Aurelius wrote that he was a citizen of the world, not of Rome. Philosophers such as Kant have held similar views. According to William F. Frankena (1965), Kant insisted that "any educational system must teach the virtues of the good man, not just those of the citizen of the country in which it operates; in the second place, he [Kant] is maintaining that in doing so it must be internationalistic in its inspiration and look to the whole future of humanity" (p. 103).

Early reconstructionists identified the need for global thinking. For example, Kilpatrick (1926) held that "Nothing less than world-mindedness will suffice—the ability to see social problems on the scale on which they exist" (p. 71). A few years later the *Educational Frontier* included the need for a worldview in its content. Hullfish wrote: "[The student] must likewise be sensitized to the fact of international interdependence in the world situation" (p. 160). This view was, quite likely, a result of the world-wide depression of the times. Nicholas Murray Butler, addressing the American Club in Paris in 1931, stated: "What I ask for, gentlemen, is a plan, a plan of international cooperation to solve the problems that have become international" (quoted in Beard, *America Faces the Future*, p. 19). Shortly thereafter, the 1934 Report of the Commission of the Social Studies concluded that there was a need to understand the problems of humankind and the importance of international relations: "This excludes any commitment of education to either a narrow or an aggressive nationalism and involves a recognition of the fact that any effective world organization must grow with an organization of national and regional unities and with domestic control of outward thrusts of economic, naval, and military power" (p. 41).

Such thought appears to have been given widespread attention in educational circles. In 1930, E.L. Thorndike and A.I. Gates in *Elementary Principles of Education* held: "A fundamental principle of education, then, is that the best in life is not to be achieved by strivings for the individual aggrandizement of a person, race, nation or any other group, but on the contrary, by striving for the advancement of [humankind] as a whole" (cited in Berkson, 1943, p. 241). The reference to striving for the advancement of humanity as a whole implies the idea of interdependence, the second point in this discussion on world community.

Interdependence is a common theme for reconstructionists. Some reconstructionists, especially Brameld, referred to Edward Bellamy's nineteenth century utopian novel *Looking Backward* in which the idea of interdependence had been put into practice:

> The great nations of Europe, as well as Australia, Mexico, and parts of South America, are now industrial republics like the United States, which was the pioneer of the evolution. The peaceful relations of these nations are assured by a loose form of federal union of world-wide extent. (p. 138)

Along with Brameld, Berkson (1943) believed that interdependence was replacing independence, and that the value of the individual would not be diminished in the process: "In the term 'interdependence' the idea of autonomy of the individual is retained, but it is united with the idea of organic relation with the community" (p. 320). In this organic relation, Paul Nash (1973) held that reconstructionists "operate on the assumption that not only is there enough for everyone but that human resources become greater if shared" (p. 352).

Reconstructionists not only stress the concept of interdependence, but also international authority as a means to design and support it. Berkson (1943) stressed the need for such authority: "The concepts of interdependence and social control lead inevitably to the idea of an international authority" (p. 321). The idea was expressed even earlier in this country by Manning (1798), in his discussion of "Organization of the Many" with a world view:

> And I have often had it impressed on my mind that in some such way as this Society might be organized throughout the world as well as government, & by sotial corraspondance & mutual consestions all differences might be settled, so that wars might be bannished from the Earth. (cited by Counts, 1938, pp. 180-181)

The concept of interdependence and international authority do not negate the need for individual nations. Berkson's (1943) position included an emphasis upon the role of strong nations: "In the new conception of world society, the nation retains a key position" (p. 321). In an earlier work, *Preface to an Educational Philosophy* (1940), Berkson explained the importance of both nation and nations by explaining the difference between cosmopolitanism and internationalism: "The former denies the value of nationality or at best places no emphasis on it; the latter makes the nation the very unit of world society, conceiving each nation as an equal member of the family of nations, emphasizing their mutual dependence, aiming to subject each nation to an international law" (pp. 162-163).

The reconstructionist's desire for world community and world government is consistent with the reconstructionist's view of democracy which looks forward to a unity of humankind. Alexander Meiklejohn (1942) expressed the view within a theological framework. The reconstructionist would refer to this as the ethical framework of democracy:

> The village belongs to the town, the town to the country, the country to the state, the state to the nation, the nation to—what? At each step in this progression a governing state finds itself governed. The lesser units are, by their own choice, bound together into a larger unit. No one of them, therefore, has more than a local sovereignty. The only sovereignty which could be unlimited would be that of a total group which includes in one organic, governing whole, all beings who are capable of joining in the common enterprise of living reasonably. To be reasonable at the highest level would be to live as a member of that all-inclusive state. If, following the suggestion which theology has given us, we assume that all normal human beings are fitted for membership in that fellowship of government then the task of civilization will be seen to be that of transforming all humanity into "a sovereign people." The human race is, in virtue of its intelligence, its kindness, a state in the making. (p. 260)

Brameld (*Toward,* 1956) held that the concept of a world community united through world government is nothing more, nor less, than the traditional idea of being good neighbors. He reminded readers that however well-meant the ideas of world community and world government may be, in reality they have not yet been accepted in practice on a world scale. The ultimate purpose remains: "To expose the conflict between the demands of traditional national sovereignty and the need for responsible international order, and to commit ourselves unequivocally to world government and world citizenship, is not only one of our highest educational obligations; it is the most urgent of those obligations" (p. 171).

Later in his career, Brameld published *The Teacher as World Citizen,* primarily a series of lectures, referring to Albert Einstein who proposed a parallel concept:

"The world is heading for atomic war." The only solution, he held, is "an effective supranational world government to which military power will be transferred." (p. x)

It may be interesting to note that Einstein's statement was made in 1947, during the years when Brameld was formulating his ideas.

As a reconstructionist, Brameld (1964) saw education as a means to bring about this world government: "In reiterating here my plea that world civilization become a *galvanizing* purpose (emphasis his) of the public schools, I mean that it is only this kind of commitment to the future life of [humankind] which can now give unity and vitality of our educational policies and program" (p. 168). This ultimate purpose of "changing the world" appeared in Brameld's *Design for America* (1945) and continued throughout his writing career. In one of the last books, *The Climactic Decade* (1970), Brameld added an appendix in which he offered a "Summary of reconstructionism." In that summary he reiterated his theme from the 1940s: "What kind of world do we want, and how can we achieve it?" (p. 199). Brameld proposed that the entire course of study be integrated around this one question. The world view is emphasized.

A more recent view is expressed by SER, which refers to the idea of world community in one of its four central concepts: GLOBAL ORDER. Learning processes that respect human dignity and diversity are advocated by SER. Its members seek ways to end exploitation, violence, and nuclear proliferation. SER helps its members to go beyond narrow ideological and national allegiances to form a global outlook encompassing all humanity.

Marshall McLuhan, in the 1960s, seemed to be bringing attention to the idea of the unity of humankind through his concept of the "global village." It should be noted that the idea was only being popularized through McLuhan, for reconstructionists had already voiced the concept. For example, in 1962 Counts wrote: "Perhaps the greatest of...all is the fact that the earth has become a 'little neighborhood' and is growing smaller by the minute" (p. 30).

Mumford, referred to previously as influencing reconstructionist thought, provided a mid-twentieth century worldview:

Let us make one basic assumption: the destiny of [humankind], after its long preparatory period of separation and differentiation, is at last to become one. Our survey of [human] successive transformations has disclosed the fact that the widening of the base of human community, though fitful and erratic, has nevertheless been one of the cumulative results of human history. This unity is on the point of being politically expressed in a world government that will unite nations and regions in transactions beyond their individual capacity; it will be spurred to these difficult tasks of political and economic unification by common ideals of human development. The words that G.A. Borgese applied to one aspect of this movement may now be applied to the whole task of building a world culture: "It is necessary; therefore it is possible." And one may add: If it were easy, it would hardly be necessary. (p. 184)

The plans for an economically united Europe, and the call for democracy in nations of the former Soviet Union, serve to support Mumford's prophetic mid-century statement. For reconstructionists, it is merely "cultural-lag" coming up to speed with reconstructionist thought. Brameld (*Explosive,* 1965) referred to the concept of *cultural lag,* crediting sociologist William F. Ogburn.

Ozman summarized the reconstructionist position by describing reconstructionists as those who

believe that we must learn to look at human affairs not in terms of any particular nation or culture, but from a worldwide point of view. They feel that such concepts as nationalism and patriotism often do more harm than good in making [humans] ethnocentric and parochial and in creating divisions...." (p. 151)

Stanley and Benne in "Social Reconstructionism for 21st-century Educators" (1995) reflect Ozman's perspective:

We argue for the eventual institutionalization of participative social planning over all the earth. Significant social and cultural changes under the direction of such an ideal set Herculean tasks for postmodern re-education. (p. 144)

The idea of a global mindset with a need for world government is based on the concept of interdependence which has been referred to earlier in this discussion. The interdependence theme is more specifically addressed in the following discussion on the reciprocal relationship of the individual and community.

> **Action in the classroom:** Students and I are establishing internet contacts with students and faculty in a French school.

Individual and Community

The emphasis upon both self and society is evident in Dewey's early writing, such as *My Pedagogic Creed:*

> I believe that this conception has due regard for both the individualistic and socialistic ideals. It is duly individual because it recognizes the formation of a certain character as the only genuine basis of right living. It is socialistic because it recognizes that this right character is not to be formed by merely individual precept, example, or exhortation, but rather by the influence of a certain form of institutional or community life upon the individual, and that the social organism through the school, as its organ, may determine ethical results. (Cremin, p. 30)

The relationship of the individual to society is given special consideration in the field of social-psychology, particularly through the work of George Mead. In *Mind, Self & Society* (1934), Mead emphasized the dual nature of self and society. Brameld (*Patterns,* 1950) referred to Mead's mind as "one of the most brilliant," strongly influencing Dewey, and suggested that Mead and Dewey provided the pioneering work in "developing the concept of the social self" (pp. 104 & 201). Within the discussion of the relationship of the self and the society, a question emerged. How does the individual develop? It would seem logical to suggest that since a group is composed of individuals, one must begin with the individual. Mead's thinking pointed to the individual arising out of the group, referring to the contract theory in this explanation:

> The contract theory of society assumes that the individuals are first all there as intelligent individuals, as selves, and that these individuals get together and form society. On this view societies have arisen like business corporations, by the deliberate coming-together of a group of investors, who elect their officers and constitute themselves a society. The individuals come first and the societies arise out of the mastery of certain individuals. The theory is an old one and in some of its phases is still current. If, however, the position

to which I have been referring is a correct one, if the individual reaches his self only through communication with others, only through the elaboration of society processes by means of significant communication, then the self could not antedate the social organism. The latter would have to be there first. (p. 233)

Mead used an analogy from biology which serves as an aid in understanding the process of individual development and the social process:

> It cannot be said that the individuals come first and the community later, for the individuals arise in the very process itself, just as much as the human body or any multi-cellular form is one in which differentiated cells arise. There has to be a life-process going on in order to have the differentiated cells; in the same way there has to be a social process going on in order that there may be individuals. (p. 189)

Mead's position was in agreement with the ideas of Counts proposed two years earlier. In *Dare the School Build a New Social Order?*, Counts emphasized culture, or society, asserting that the individual is given the freedom to become an individual only by being born into a culture. A previous reference has been made to Counts' idea, but it is offered here again to underscore: (1) The reconstructionist view of the relationship between the individual and community; and (2) The importance of community in developing the individual:

> There is the fallacy that man is born free. As a matter of fact, he is born helpless. He achieves freedom, as a race and as an individual, through the medium of culture. The most crucial of all circumstances conditioning human life is birth into a particular culture. (p. 13)

Mead related the issue to reconstruction, both individual and social. His view was that they were reciprocal. According to Mead, social reconstruction included self-reconstruction and vice versa. Since the self was a product of the social, one could not change the self without changing what he called the social order: "Social reconstruction and self or personality reconstruction are the two sides of a single process—the process of human social evolution" (p. 309).

Such a viewpoint leads reconstructionists to propose an education that places emphasis on both the individual and society. While Mead and Counts published their ideas, Rugg (1931) called for an educational theory which would "embrace the coordinate concepts—

'the individual' and 'the social.'" (p. 252). During the same period, Kandel (1930), though not a reconstructionist, reminded readers of the shift in thinking from an emphasis on the individual in the nineteenth century to "something more" in the twentieth: "Something more is needed, and that is active consciousness on the part of the individual that in return for these rights [s/he] owes certain duties and obligations to society and his country in the form of active cooperation and interest in the promotion of its welfare" (p. 84).

In succeeding years Raup and his associates (1950) called attention to the need to recognize responsibility to both self and society, discussing the paradoxical nature of the issue:

> [Humanity] has wrestled with this seeming paradox for many centuries and has made [its] worst mistakes when...[seeking] to emphasize exclusively either the integrity of the individual or the integrity of the group. [Humanity] seems to have been wisest when...willing to face the seemingly paradoxical claims of both and has tried to get along with both of them. The only other choice has been to find wholeness in the imaginatively made society of another world. But this third claimant does not command the acceptance of our age. The integration we seek lies for us in the continual adjustment to each other of the two complementary and mutually dependent processes of development—that of the individual and that of the social community. It seems correct, and it is the proper argument of democracy, to hold that there is more real integrity in the social order when each, the individual and the community, is developed in its own right and yet with the profoundest provisions for the integrity of the other. (p. 261)

Somewhat later, Brameld (*Cultural,* 1955) continued with this emphasis upon a democracy which respected the integrity of both the individual and the community. He followed the theory that individual development is only possible through the group. The ideas of Mead and Counts are evident in Brameld's explanation:

> In order that the individual may become a self at all [the individual] must actively participate in a community of selves. Accurately speaking, the infant is not born a personality. [The infant] becomes one gradually as [s/he] is made conscious of [her/his] self by becoming conscious of other personalities. This occurs as the young child learns to communicate—a process that involves the anticipation of responses that others will make to [her/his] vocal, written, overt gesture. Through these responses [s/he] discovers

that there are other selves and that [s/he], too, is a self with similar desires and capacities. (p. 114)

This development, indeed, optimum development of both individual and community, became a major emphasis in Brameld's view of Educational Reconstruction. Rather than merely referring to this as freedom, Brameld coined his own term: social-self-realization. For Brameld, this was the ultimate; it was the all-embracing, all-encompassing, supreme value. This concept went beyond Abraham Maslow's self-actualization, for the emphasis of Maslow was clear: the self. Brameld (1970) stressed a dual emphasis, a reciprocity, an interdependence: "Self and society are *reciprocal* [emphasis his]; neither is regarded as the sufficient cause of the other" (p. 109).

In trying to understand Brameld's concept of social-self-realization, it is helpful to review the different works of Brameld since specific texts offer different perspectives or descriptions. For example, in *Education as Power* Brameld used the image of communion: "It means, in essence, the ever-growing fulfillment of the powers of [individuals] in communion with other [individuals]" (p. 59). This same theme is offered earlier in the text: "It is the realization of the capacity of the self to measure up to its fullest, most satisfying powers in cooperative relationship with other selves" (p. 48). The continued emphasis on both the individual and the relationship to others is a common theme.

Brameld's "Education for What?," condensed in *The Education Digest* (1956), provides additional clarity to the concept of social-self-realization. Among the literature reviewed for this study, this excerpt appears to be the nearest to a definition that Brameld provided:

> All normal people want to achieve a number of goals—some of them physiological, some psychological, some social. They want to be adequately nourished, for example. They want security. They want to work at something that gives them satisfaction. They want to be appreciated and loved. They want to feel that they belong to an enterprise larger than themselves to which they can give their loyalty. They want to participate in determining the conditions by which they live. There are still other goals, of course, and each can be stated in somewhat different words. But all tend to fuse together toward one overarching goal. They might be called "social-self-realization"—a term which symbolizes the desire of most [people] for the richest possible fulfillment of themselves both personally

and in their relations with other [individuals] through groups and institutions. (p. 21)

It may be noted that the three words forming Brameld's concept are hyphenated, forming one idea. T.M. Thomas (1989), a student of Brameld, recalled a class session in which Brameld made a specific note, pointing out that the hyphens were used to emphasize the inter-relatedness of the three separate concepts and their fusion into one.

Nobuo Shimahara (1973), another student of Brameld's, used a metaphor in describing social-self-realization, referring to it as "our bifocal vision of culture-and-personality" (p. 10). The hyphenation may be noted; its form is parallel to Brameld's social-self-realization.

As in previous sections, Ozman's description of reconstruction serves as a summary. In this excerpt, Ozman emphasized the concept that the person can only become an individual through society:

> Reconstructionists emphasize that individuals and society should be partners in an enterprise wherein one aids the other, and that society and [humanity] are engaged in a symbiotic relationship. Reconstructionists insist that the development of the individual must go hand in hand with the development of society—that people can only truly become individuals when their talents and capacities are used to improve the world in which they live. (p. 149)

Within the framework of an emphasis upon a reciprocity between individual and community, upon world community and world government, and upon the democratic process, there is a theme which runs through all. The theme is the reconstructionist respect, not only for the individual, but more specifically, a continual championing of common humanity in society.

Action in the classroom: Students identify experiences in which they achieved both individual and group fulfillment in their families and other groups of which they are members.

The Common People in Society

One of the four concepts which shape the goals of SER is "cooperative power." In the description of this concept there is a reference to "change activists" and "overcoming the evil effects of ageism, racism, sexism, and other types of unfair discrimination."

The groups experiencing evil effects are often subjected to the authority of another group. Reconstructionists are concerned with those who seem to be exploited or in powerless positions. This draws reconstructionists to become involved in efforts as "change agents" or "social activists."

Bode, in *Modern Educational Theories* (1927), devoted the first chapter to "The American Tradition of Democracy." His explanation of democracy concluded with the "faith in the common":

> No one, not even the humblest citizen, is to serve simply as a hewer of wood and a drawer of water, but everyone is to be recognized as a member of a great brotherhood, and to share in the opportunities, the achievements, and the aspirations which are our common possession. There are to be no peasants, no serfs, as there are no hereditary privileges and titles, because each citizen is to rise to the full stature of [his/her] spiritual manhood even as a [son/daughter] in [his/her] father's house. So runs our national creed. It is a creed that is based on faith in *the common*..." [emphasis added], a faith that does not shrink from comparison with the glory that was Greece or the splendor that was Rome. (p. 9)

The fact remains that American society has not lived up to the creed which Bode described. Although the terms *peasants* and *serfs* are not a part of the American vocabulary, the images they represent can be found without difficulty. The growing number of homeless is one example. As a result, reconstructionists continue this interest in "the common." Such interest is consistent with the reconstructionist emphasis upon crises discussed earlier. Even though the Cold War is reported to have ended, reconstructionists perceive other crises with equally devastating potential and that common needs persist.

In *Patterns of Educational Philosophy*, Brameld discussed the role of the common people in three periods of history, summarizing the power that the common achieved in the ancient, medieval, and modern cultures. In *Ends and Means in Education,* Brameld perceived the continuing influence of the common people who demanded and won their rights, believing that education could be the power that could achieve a world community in which there "should emerge nothing less than control of the industrial system, of public services, and of cultural and natural resources by and for the common people who, throughout the ages, have struggled for a life of security, decency, and peace for themselves and their children" (p. 17).

The emphasis that reconstructionists place on aiding those with little or no authority to improve their conditions is also evident in later reconstructionist writing. An example is Thomas' reference (1985) to the work of Brazilian educator Paulo Freire, cited in the earlier discussion on indoctrination. In referring to Freire, Thomas explained education's role:

> Education has a central role to play in promoting such an aware-ness among oppressed people. This innovative function focusing on social transformation is one of the central themes of reconstruc-tionism. (p. 11)

The roots of the reconstructionist idea of "education as a central role in promoting awareness among oppressed people" can be found in the early twentieth century in such examples as Caroline Pratt's City and Country School in Greenwich Village. Susan F. Semel (1995) describes Pratt's active learning methods:

> What emerged from this model was a community of independent young children who were actively engaged in their learning, while concurrently contributing to the life of their school community. In sum, these students were, to return to Dewey, "saturated with the spirit of service," while learning to be self-directed in the context of the school community—" (pp. 94-95)

The roots of the present practice of service-learning—a learning method which exemplifies reconstructionist thought—are evident in Pratt's school.

Two decades later, the reconstructionist idea of radical change in community through action of teachers was evident in the work of African-American educators in Virginia. According to Michael James in "Southern Progressivism and the Great Depression, "...seizing the ideology and language of the social reconstructionists, African-American educators in Virginia were able to carve out for themselves a tenuous foothold in state educational policymaking" (p. 115).

Reconstructionist work by African Americans has continued throughout the twentieth century. For example, Dean Yarbrough, a charter member of SER and former principal in the Boston Public Schools, has consistently brought attention to the violation of human rights. In a Memorial Day address at Sudbury, Massachusetts (1996), Yarbrough focused on human rights and profits:

Our vision of human rights has been displaced by high profits. High profits for *few* Americans, lower wages for American workers whose jobs have been moved, for example, to China.

Today the enemies are not all foreign military powers. One of the threats is the gradual displacement of our focus on freedom and human rights by the focus on profits. We see more and more products that are made in China which has a deplorable human rights record. ...And yet, China has been designated a most favored nation trading status. I consider this to be a moral disgrace! This weakening of our concepts of freedom and human rights is a threat to our security just as much as a foreign military threat.

Along with an activist interest in the welfare of the common people, reconstructionists believe in the wisdom of the common. This is in keeping with the reconstructionist view of social democracy. Brameld (*Power,* 1965) implied the wisdom of common humanity when he issued this challenge:

Test yourself: if you want to see the principle of political bipolarity extended to world civilization, you believe that you, in concert with your fellows all over the world, are the final, ultimate judges of what is best for you. You are the ones to establish policy—no minority, no super-authority, no special-interest group—only you. Thus you must have faith not only in yourself but in your fellow citizens. If you possess this faith, you believe in democracy; if you do not possess it, you do not believe in democracy regardless of the words you use. (p. 37)

Brameld's description of democracy relates to the reconstructionist twofold interest in the common people as discussed earlier in this section. First, the common often have no authority, and second, the common must have the ability to make decisions for their own benefit. The latter provides the rationale for reconstructionists emphasis on social democracy. The interpretation of democracy evident in Brameld's statement above encourages social activism; it has resulted in reconstructionists often being referred to as radical.

The term *radical* is one which reconstructionists use to describe themselves, and it is also used by others to characterize reconstructionists. However, the reconstructionist meaning of radical differs from that which is commonly used; the reconstructionist interpretation relates to the concepts of the future and utopia, combined in the following discussion.

Action in the classroom: Students identify situations in which they perceive themselves as being powerless, explaining feelings and thoughts. Is anyone helping? Who could and isn't?

Radicalism, Futurism, Utopianism

The interrelatedness of the concepts of radicalism, futurism, and utopianism is explained by Shimahara (1987); he defines the meaning of *radical* in the context of reconstructionist philosophy:

> When used in this context, it refers to utopia, the ideal. Its focus is on what does not exist, on what is to be.

There are references to all three concepts. Shimahara relates *radical* to *utopia,* then infers to the *future* by "what does not exist...what is to be." Shimahara's statement is representative of the way in which the concepts are used in reconstructionist writing.

As mentioned earlier, reconstructionists often refer to their philosophy as being internally radical, and the activistic nature of reconstructionists sometimes results in their being referred to as radicals. For example, when Harold J. Laski (1936) wrote "a comment in a general way" about the 1934 report of the Commission on the Social Studies, he expressed concern about how the business community would interpret the report or the implementation of the ideas in the report. Laski commented:

> When the business men translate this request into concrete terms, what does it mean? Radicals in the schools. (p. 344)

Laski's use of the term implies that the business community would necessarily view the ideas expressed in the report as negative.

There is a difference in how reconstructionists use the term when referring to the philosophy and their actions, and how others sometimes use the term when referring to reconstructionist philosophy or the actions of reconstructionists. Both may be using the same term to describe the same situation, but with different meanings.

When the term *radical* is used by those "outside" of reconstructionist philosophy to define or describe the philosophy, it often has a critical or negative connotation, as the Laski example indicates. What appears to occur is that the change which reconstructionist philosophy and action produces may be viewed as undesirable. More specifically, the undesirable change may appear to be too quick or too extreme, and the speed and its departure from the normative are viewed negatively. The changes are conceived of as activities carried out by "extremists" or "radicals." The reconstructionists may view the same situation as a values idea. For example, Conrad (1987) states, "Reconstructionism would be considered a normative philosophy."

The reconstructionist view of radical is not a recently developed one. By 1940 and perhaps earlier, the philosophy appears to have had a reputation for being radical. In *Preface to an Educational Philosophy* (1940), Berkson made reference to *The Educational Frontier* (1933), stating that the publication represented the position of the reconstructionists and that "despite more radical connotations associated with 'reconstructionist' educational philosophy, it is the American tradition which is at the basis, not any conception of a new hypothetical or experimental social order" (pp. 51-52). Two interpretations of radical are implied in Berkson's statement: "radical connotations" meaning "extremist"; "American tradition" meaning "root."

Brameld (1977) emphasized these aspects of the concept. First, he reminded readers of Webster's generic meaning: "from the roots, going to the foundation, basic" (p. 67)). If we look carefully at Brameld's beliefs regarding concepts such as democracy and freedom, we can see that he referred to the root meanings. For example, Brameld held that the Jeffersons, Franklins, and Paines were all genuine radicals.

The second meaning of radical, according to Brameld, is a focus on the future. Brameld indicated this emphasis in his position when he stated that being radical meant "to be future-directed, exploratory in hitherto untried directions of history." Another of Brameld's references (*Power,* 1965) makes the same point:

> "We must reshape. We must renew the culture. Otherwise we are lost." In a precise sense, this is the viewpoint of radicalism. (p. 24)

Present-day reconstructionists are grounded in the idea of radicalism as understood to mean both "going to the root" and "looking to the future." Conrad's comment regarding the normative nature of reconstruction indicates his view of "going to the root." Similarly, Shimahara (1973) wrote: "By *radical* is meant going to the root, asking fundamental questions" (p. 10). The second meaning, "looking to the future," is evident in Ozman's appraisal of reconstruction when he asserted that, "There is no denying that, basically, reconstructionists are future-oriented and optimistic people" (p. 146).

A belief in the power of the human mind and the impact that one's thinking processes can have over what is emerging leads reconstructionists to focus on the future. Reconstructionists believe that humankind can determine its own future. Brameld (1973) quoted Warren W. Wager who argued:

> Within the unknowable final limits of human nature, we shall go where we please, as far as we choose to see. The ultimate function of prophecy is not to tell the future, but to make it. (p. 30)

Brameld closed his article, citing I.F. Stone:

> I think every [person] is [their] own Pygmalion, and spends...life fashioning [themselves]. And in fashioning...for good or ill...fashions the human race and its future. (p. 35)

Mumford, in *The Transformation of Man*, wrote in a similar vein but used a different metaphor. His image is much like Shakespeare's "all the world's a stage," but with greater definition:

> Man begins as an actor, detached from his animal colleagues, already something of a star performer, but uncertain of what part he shall learn. In time, he becomes a scene painter, modifying the natural background and finding his own part modified by it, too: and he is driven to be a stagehand, likewise, shifting the "properties" to make his entrances and exits more manageable. Only after much practice in all these roles, as scene painter, stagehand, costumer, make-up artist, actor, does man discover that his main function is to write and direct the drama. In composing the play itself man uses, in Shakespearean fashion, many of the old plots left by nature, but he gives them a new turn of the imagination and works the events up to a climax that nature, without his aid, might not have blundered upon for countless million years. (p. 238)

Humankind's ability to determine the future as described by Mumford raised a question: What kind of future? Reconstructionists would respond by saying, "a utopian future." Like the term *radical*, *utopian* carries a double meaning. Reconstructionists use the term in a specific way. For example, Shimahara's statement at the opening of this section made reference to "the ideal," "what does not exist," "what is to be."

It may be important to note that reconstructionists do not define *utopian* as the impossible, the unrealistic, or as fantasy, which are common alternative interpretations. The view of reconstructionists is that *utopian* means that which is possible. References have been made to Bellamy's nineteenth-century novel *Looking Backward,* which reconstructionists refer to as an example of their view of utopia. Bellamy speaks of the possible.

Brameld (*Explosive,* 1965) cited Karl Mannheim as another example. According to Brameld,

> Mannheim is not referring to an escape from reality—to castles in the air or dreams of heaven on earth. Rather, the utopian attitude is, in Hegelian terms, a kind of dialectical polarity to the ideological attitude. It may, indeed, function both as critique of and corrective for the obsolescences and distortions that it discovers in the ideological portrait of a given culture. (p. 151)

Jay M. Smith refers to a reconstructionist view of utopia in SER's *Global Images of Peace and Education.* The book concludes: "Members of The Society for Educational Reconstruction are utopians who envision a world of peace, brotherhood, equality and freedom" (p. 276). Reconstruction suggests that all of these visions are attainable; indeed, they must be attained if humankind is to survive. Benne and Stanley (1995) reinforce the reconstructionist view of attainable dreams: "Direct democracy can no longer rationally be dismissed as a figment of social reconstructionists' imagination, their impossible dream" (p. 166).

To summarize, the terms *radical, future,* and *utopian* carry specific meanings for reconstructionists. While critics may employ the terms to describe their disagreement with reconstructionist ideas or practices, reconstructionists use them to describe the same goals and practices that Educational Reconstruction supports. Inherent in the reconstructionists' view of *radial, future,* and *utopia* is change. Since reconstructionists are sensitive to continuing crises that exist, they view change as a necessity in order to improve existing conditions. Although there have already been numerous references to the concept of change in this study, the following discussion is particularly devoted to this concept.

> **Action in the classroom:** Students relate experiences—theirs
> and others, in which establishing a vision served as a means
> to bring the vision into reality.

Change

Early reconstructionist thought centered on the subject of change.
Kilpatrick addressed "The Fact of Rapid Change and Its Demands"
in *Education for a Changing Civilization* (1926). Since he believed
that change was a fact, he argued that a philosophy must be one of
change:

> In our actual world of affairs, we must with Darwin look backward
> and forward into ceaseless and, so far as we can tell to the contrary,
> all-inclusive change. We must agree with James—our universe is
> wide open, the lid is off. We face an unknown future, not fixed as
> to goal. Whether we like it or no, a philosophy of change is the only
> one that can so deal with our world as to give us guidance. (p. 83)

Kilpatrick's idea of "all inclusive change" is a reminder of the reconstructionist holistic position.

The earlier illustration of Brameld's view of education and
culture may be recalled: education as a central circle, touching all
other circles of culture. With that illustration, Brameld (*Explosive*,
1965) asserted that no culture is ever static, that there is a continual
evolutionary process. He referred to Sir Julian Huxley's position:
"Evolution in the most general terms is a natural process of irrevers-
ible change, which generates novelty, variety, and increase of organization: and all reality can be regarded in one aspect as evolution" (pp.
165-166.) The process of change can be understood through a review
of the three stages of evolution: the preorganic, organic, and the
postorganic.

The preorganic stage is composed of nonliving matter such as
rocks and stars; the organic stage includes living matter such as plants
and animals; the postorganic stage involves human behavior. Brameld
(*Power*, 1965) pointed out the unique aspect about the latter stage
and its relationship to human responsibility:

> Now the extraordinary fact about the postorganic stage is that it is
> the only one of the three not entirely the result of blind forces in

nature. Only it, in other words, contains within it the power of conscious awareness with which [humanity], alone among earthly species, is endowed. Through it [humanity] remembers the mistakes...made in the past and imagines ways in which to prevent them in the future. [Humanity] alone, in short, is the evolution-directing animal. (p. 129)

If humanity is "the evolution-directing animal" as Brameld held, then reconstructionists ask why change should not be directed. According to Brameld (1970), "[Humanity] alone possesses the capacity to be aware of and to engage in [its] own deliberate development" (p. 109). Humanity directing change is evident in Stone's view of three types of change (1987):

Reconstructionism asserts that change is an ever-present fact. Now there are several ways of viewing change. There is the change without human intervention. Then there is change planned by a small minority; this seems to be the most common—a few individuals determine what will happen to the larger group. Or there can be educational reconstructionism—a method of introducing ideas to citizens; there is participation, such as anthropotherapy.[3]

The "ever-present fact" of change mentioned by Stone is evident in the thinking of another of Brameld's former students, Gertrude F. Langsam (1987):

Society changes; education changes. This, of course, comes from Dewey. He used the analogy of "you never put the child in the same bath water twice" [first said by Heraclitus]. He used images of water. When you go swimming, the water is never the same. Nature, environment keeps changing. It is being reconstructed. And in the human environment, there is constant change; sociologically, it has to.

Reconstructionists, in summary, believe that change is inescapable and that the human species has the capability and responsibility to direct it. Reconstruction philosophy is a means to give guidance to the process of change. The interplay of process and product relates to the next tenet which focuses on the interplay of ends and means. The change which reconstructionists wish to make is designed by determining both the results of the desired change as well as determining the methods to achieve those results.

> **Action in the classroom:** Students identify a change they would like to develop in their conduct, the classroom, or the school and develop a plan for change. Visioning and imaging techniques are appropriate.

Goal Orientation: Ends and Means

While Educational Reconstruction accepts the importance of action, it holds that action, by itself, is not enough; action must be guided by desired ends. Reconstruction is considered a goal-oriented philosophy.

The attention to ends is evident in the writings of Dewey. In *Democracy and Education* (1916), he referred to Plato's interest in the ends (goals) of existence. Dewey continued: "Unless we know the end, the good, we shall have no criterion for rationally deciding what the possibilities are which should be promoted, nor how social arrangments [*sic*] are to be ordered" (p. 103).

Counts, likewise, emphasized the need for attention to direction. Counts is representative of those who believed that progressivism was placing too much emphasis on action and too little on direction. The following excerpt from *Dare the School Build a New Social Order?* employs an analogy which indicates the extreme to which he believed action without direction had been taken. Because of the uniqueness and force of Counts' description, it is presented here in its entirety:

> If an educational movement, or any other movement, calls itself progressive, it must have orientation; it must possess direction. The word itself implies moving forward, and moving forward can have little meaning in the absence of clearly defined purposes. We cannot like Stephen Leacock's horseman, dash off in all directions at once. Nor should we, like our presidential candidates, evade every disturbing issue and be all things to all men. Also we must beware lest we become so devoted to motion that we neglect the question of direction and be entirely satisfied with movement in circles. Here, I think, we find the fundamental weakness, not only of Progressive Education, but also of American education generally. Like a baby shaking a rattle, we seem to be utterly content with action, providing it is sufficiently vigorous and noisy. In the last analysis a very large part of American educational thought, inquiry, and experimentation is much ado about nothing. And, if we

are permitted to push the analogy of the rattle a bit further, our consecration to motion is encouraged and supported in order to keep us out of mischief. At least we know that so long as we thus busy ourselves we shall not incur the serious displeasure of our social elders. (pp. 6-7)

The importance of orientation, direction, and purpose as expressed by Counts was not unique to those in education. Other writers called attention to the need for awareness of ends. T.V. Smith in *The Democratic Way of Life* reminded readers: "[Humanity] is capable of becoming an end-guided, rather than a mere pressure-propelled animal" (p. 71).

The interest in action and aim, or means and ends, became important during the Depression years and following. Because of the economic disaster, discussion focused on planning in order to avoid such a disaster again. For example, Butler, in the address referred to previously, stated, "Gentlemen, if we wait too long, somebody will come forward with a solution that we may not like." The inference is that there must be planning, perhaps even "a plan" (Beard, 1932, p. 16).

It was the fear of "a plan" which raised questions such as: Who would develop "the plan"? The result was a debate on whether to have a "planning society" or a "planned society." Dewey and Childs in *The Educational Frontier* provided the perspective of what was to become the reconstructionist position:

Russia and Italy both present us with patterns of planned societies. We believe profoundly that society requires planning; that planning is the alternative to chaos, disorder, and insecurity. But there is a difference between a society which is plann*ed* and a society which is continuously plann*ing*—namely, the difference between autocracy and democracy, between dogma and intelligence in operation, between suppression of individuality and that release and utilization of individuality which will bring it to full maturity. (p. 72)

As the issue continued to be discussed, reconstructionists concluded that there must be what Raup and associates called, "the continuity of means and ends" (p. 1660). Dewey and Childs (*Underlying Philosophy*, 1933) pointed out the reciprocity that must occur between ends and means:

> A goal cannot be intelligently set forth apart from the path which leads to it. Ends cannot be conceived as operative ends, as directors of action, apart from consideration of conditions which obstruct and means which promote them. If stated at large, apart from means, ends are empty. (p. 296)

The preceding quotation provides some interesting speculation. It is very probable that Brameld was influenced by such thought since he ultimately used the same language as Dewey and Childs. For example, one of Brameld's first major works is entitled *Ends and Means in Education* (1950), evidence of his emphasis on the concept. Brameld explained the interplay between the two, indicating that the end affects the functions needed to accomplish the result, and that the functions may continuously change and determine the outcome. Brameld's conclusion is provided in his well-known couplet:

> Ends without means are empty,
> but means without ends are blind. (p. 239)

Obviously, the preceding is based on Kant's aphorism:

> Precepts without concepts are empty,
> concepts without precepts are blind.

Reconstructionists echo yet another root of Kantian thought, that of the relationship of ends and means to individuals. Kant (cited in Frankena) gave the following advice which is also at the heart of Educational Reconstruction:

> Act so that you treat humanity, whether in your own person or in that of another, always as an end and never as a means only. (p. 108)

Kantian thought relates to discussions in two previous sections in this chapter. The first is Kant's emphasis upon the importance of the individual which appears to be at the root of the social ethic held by reconstructionists as discussed in the section on democracy. The second is the emphasis on both means and ends in the process of change which indicates the philosophic framework of holism as discussed in the opening of this chapter.

Since reconstruction is considered a goal-oriented philosophy, questions emerge: What goals are considered worthy? Toward what is it that reconstruction directs human energies? These questions move the discussion to what reconstruction considers as truth.

> **Action in the classroom:** Students and I explore goals (ends)—personal or school-related, we are working toward. We then analyze the process (means) used in working toward the goal, noting the interplay between the goal (end) and the process of working toward the goal (means).

Truth: Tested Thought

Kilpatrick published *Education for a Changing Civilization* (1926), discussing the nature of the changing times. Immediately following that short discussion, Kilpatrick introduced the concept of "tested thought," which he considered a necessity; it is a process that reconstructionists utilize to determine truth rather than accepting pre-determined conclusions or absolutes from times and places.

A rationale for tested thought can be drawn from Galileo's experiment, or the symbolic value of it as myth. The blind acceptance which is believed to have existed prior to the Galileo experiment exemplifies what Dewey referred to when he stated, "An interest in discovery took the place of an interest in systematizing and 'proving' received beliefs." Dewey (1916) held that in such discovery thinking started: "Through its critical process true knowledge is revised and extended, and our convictions as to the state of things reorganized" (pp. 344-345). Dewey's reference to the "critical process" is the theme in this discussion of tested thought.

The idea of tested thought relates not only to drawing conclusions based on the scientific method, but in the world of ideas as well. Ideas are to be put through a "critical process" by being discussed and debated before decisions are made. The ideas must then be acted upon. For reconstructionists, an important kind of truth is not truth until it is agreed upon and acted on as explained by Brameld (*Toward,* 1956):

> Truth as social consensus then becomes, we might say, the utopian content of the "group mind." This truth is any active agreement about the dominant goals, and means for achieving them, of the culture. Such a social consensus is neither merely verbal nor static; it involves action and hence involves application of the utopian content of the "group mind" to reconstructing institutions, practices, habits, and attitudes. Although it also involves continuous

use of the canons of logic and experimentation, its ultimate truth is tested in the cultural demonstration, made possible with the aid of logic and experiment, that it produces the cultural design that it sets out to produce. In short, the kind of truths most sought by the reconstructionist are achievements of the "group mind" conceived of in two ways: first, as *means* for active progress toward its goals, and secondly as *end*, (emphasis his) in possession of its goals. (p. 107)

Brameld's statement is developed around the basic concepts of the reconstructionist view of determining "kinds of truths." Attention is given to both ends and means, and the determination of ends and means is accomplished through the process of consensus. Once that consensus is attained, it must be followed by action in the reconstructing of culture which Brameld emphasizes in *Toward a Reconstructed Philosophy of Education* (1956):

> The truths of the most vital experiences in group life within any culture are determined, not merely by the needful satisfactions they produce, but also by the extent to which their import is agreed upon and then acted upon by the largest possible number of the group concerned. Without this agreement, followed by actions that test the agreement the experience simply is not "true." (pp. 92-93)

Brameld's use of quotation marks around *true* indicates that "truth" may not be a truth for all times and all places; it is not accepted as an absolute but always open to analysis and further discovery. Brameld contends there are four steps in the consensus process: presentation of evidence, communication, agreement, and action (p. 347).

Another aspect of social consensus is that it goes beyond counting noses, differentiating it from a vote which, according to Harlan Cleveland, former dean of the Humphrey Institute at the University of Minnesota, is "a snap shot in time." It is quantitative. Consensus, on the other hand, is flexible, changing, on-going. According to Brameld (*Patterns,* 1950), consensus is more qualitative:

> Let us remember that this kind of judgment is not attained simply by counting of noses; it is not primarily a *quantitative* judgment. It is also a judgment about something *qualitatively* shared—namely, about values prehended, unrational, and held in common [emphasis his]. Since these can best be epitomized by some such comprehensive value as social-self-realization, the test of majority rule is, therefore, the degree to which it creates genuinely shared policies and practices that bring social-self-realization closer to complete fulfillment. (p. 486)

The use of social consensus is broad. Although Brameld referred to it in his educational philosophy as a way of learning (*Toward*, 1956, p. 179), it has broader usage as he indicates here (*Patterns*, 1950): "It's [social consensus] concerned to build a workable process by which people can arrive at workable products in the area particularly of crucial cultural issues and choices" (p. 707).

In contrast to social consensus is the Brameldian concept of defensible partiality. Although it "rests upon the social consensus principle" (p. 705), defensible partiality has a greater educational applicability for Brameld. This conclusion is based on a statement in *The Climactic Decade* (1970):"For in a certain sense, defensible partiality is the mind and heart of the democratic ethos epitomized in educational terms" (p. 188). Brameld explains the concept:

> By it, I mean that democratic learning consists of searching for answers to the most pressing human problems through comparative investigation of as many alternative approaches as are available—always with a view to arriving at the most plausible, in the sense of evidentially grounded and cooperatively attained, conclusions that such investigations can provide. The partialities that then emerge (they may not do so in some instances because the alternatives remain too conflictive) are regarded as defensible in that they have been constructed out of a dialectic of "due process" that has exposed them to modify and correct such features, and that compels them to be supported by the strongest, most reliable testimony and agreements that are available through evidence and communication. (p. 187)

Related to both social consensus and defensible partiality is a third concept under the theme of tested thought—consensual validation. In "Values: Education's Most Neglected Problem" (1964), Brameld gave this definition:

> ...a process by which I express to others one or more of my own value preferences, each of which I define as a want-satisfaction, in the richest possible dialectic of cooperative, open, searching examination—a process by which I also seek their own evidence and reasons for sharing or not sharing in my preferences, and by which we then try to reach whatever agreements or disagreements that we can together, with a view to actions that will overtly dramatize our judgments and thereby help to check them. (p. 162)

Conrad discussed consensual validation in *Education for Trans-*

formation (1976); one may note the emphasis on process:

> To validate the consensus on this issue, members might question the sources of evidence received, and perhaps the speed at which consensus was achieved. Was intimidation or manipulation used to sway people? If so, to what extent would it invalidate the decision? Did members communicate freely? Was the decision made because it was popular or because it was morally right? What values were accepted as good and which rejected as bad or wrong? Was the consensus consistent with the larger needs of humankind? Through empirical retesting and thorough probing the consensus could become validated, or invalidated, as the case may be. The use of the Delphi Technique might prove useful to test the validity of the consensus. (p. 151)

The process emphasis echoes Brameld's thinking (1977) about consensual validation: "...a theory of experimental inquiry supplemented by much more concern for truth-seeking as an actively social or dialogic rather than so exclusively as an individualized process" (p. 70).

Defensible partiality, in summary, is primarily an education process to develop the best possible grounding or conclusion. Social consensus goes one step beyond, by requiring that ideas agreed upon must also be acted upon. Consensual validation places an emphasis not only on the social nature of the process and product, but on the quality of the process and outcome of that social nature—the ultimate goal being the common, meaning that which is held in common.

As mentioned previously, reconstructionists believe that truth is to be discovered though processes just described. If, according to the reconstructionists, truth does not pre-exist, is there any foundation, any constant within reconstructionist thought? The question moves the discussion to the subject of values.

Action in the classroom: Students and I study the Galileo story and apply the process to a discovery of truth(s) we have made.

Values

Since Educational Reconstruction is a goal-oriented philosophy and is grounded in the concept of culture, there is the question of whether there are, as Brameld mentioned, "dominant goals" or values which can be used as a framework for all peoples. As Brameld stated (*Patterns,* 1950), "We are obligated to determine as precisely as possible what values to achieve" (p. 477). Brameld attempted to determine those values; however, he considered dealing with values difficult as indicated in his discussion of values in *The Climactic Decades* with a reference to Albert Einstein:

> It is said that somebody once remarked to Albert Einstein, "Professor Einstein, you often seem to be keenly interested in political science." Einstein reportedly smiled and answered, "My friend, political science is infinitely more difficult than physics!" And no wonder, if we note that political science is one of the behavioral sciences fraught with problems of human value. (p. 96)

Berkson (1950) similarly referred to Einstein, paraphrasing Einstein's idea: "Science can provide us with objective knowledge which aids in the fulfillment of definite purposes, but it can not give us the ethical aims that characterize the human being" (p. 188). The "ethical aims" become a task for Educational Reconstruction.

If Educational Reconstruction considers the subject of values important, yet is adamant about avoiding absolutism, can it at the same time determine its dominant goals? In pursuing this question it is important to distinguish between absolutism, relativism, and universalism. Einstein's general theory of relativity, that there are no independent absolutes, is at the heart of reconstructionist thought. One could say that for the reconstructionists, the world is one of "absolute relativism." However, for those critical of such a position as ungrounded, the reconstructionist emphasis upon universalism must be taken into consideration.

While carrying on a constant vigil of examination before drawing conclusions, the reconstructionist seeks to determine universals, those values or goals which are true for most people most of the time: Are there certain values and goals which most people cherish? The key word in the previous question is *most.*

Brameld (*Toward,* 1956) developed a list of twelve goals which he suggested are universal and which, he held, could provide a framework for social reconstruction of society. It should be noted that each is introduced with the word *most.*

1. Most people do not want to be hungry; they cherish the value of *sufficient nourishment.*

2. Most people do not want to be cold or ragged; they cherish the value of *adequate dress*.

3. Most people do not want uncontrolled exposure, either to the elements or to people; they cherish the value of *shelter* and *privacy*.

4. Most people do not want celibacy; they cherish the value of *sexual expression*.

5. Most people do not want illness; they cherish the value of *physiological* and *mental health*.

6. Most people do not want chronic economic insecurity; they cherish the value of *steady work, steady income*.

7. Most people do not want loneliness; they cherish value of *companionship, mutual devotion, belongingness*.

8. Most people do not want indifference; they cherish the value of *recognition, appreciation, status*.

9. Most people do not want constant monotony, routine, or drudgery; they cherish the value of *novelty, curiosity, variation, recreation, adventure, growth, creativity*.

10. Most people do not want ignorance; they cherish the value of *literacy, skill, information*.

11. Most people do not want to be continually dominated; they cherish the value of *participation, sharing*.

12. Most people do not want bewilderment; they cherish the value of *fairly immediate meaning, significance, order, direction*. (pp. 115-116)

Brameld went on to discuss some of the complexities in determining values such as the problem of inconsistency:

Some of the values we have listed may seem to be incompatible with others. The want of security, for example, does not appear to be entirely in harmony with the want of adventure. (p. 117)

Brameld reminded the reader that what appeared to be a problem, a difficulty in determining values, was also a benefit in the process:

We must bear in mind that it is unnecessary to try to make human nature fit a single mold. Uniformity is both forlorn and colorless as an ideal. Our task is to build a culture wide enough and flexible enough to allow for the expression and satisfaction of the wide diversity of human want. (p. 118)

Reconstructionists attempt to avoid absolutism and to seek what Brameld referred to as "cultural relativism *and* universalism." Attention is given to each situation but within a framework of values and goals which seem to hold true most of the time for most of the people and which can be changed if no longer serving the best ends. Thomas (1989) indicates the reconstructionist position on values: "In regard to values—Absolutism: No. Universalism: Yes."

The role which philosophy plays in reconstructionist thinking about values can be understood in a statement by Berkson (1940):

> Philosophy is to be employed as a directive of social action, but it is to be taken as a hypothesis not as a dogma, that is, as a theory which may be modified or reconstructed in the process of putting it into practice. The application of theory to life is thus at the same time a testing out of the theory, with the likelihood of revision and the possibility of rejection. (pp. 208-209)

The testing out of the theory, according to Berkson, is through the democratic process, for it is the "ethical core of our social philosophy."

The development of character education in schools can be guided by reconstruction philosophy. What values does a community want its school to transmit to it students? The preceding statement of Berkson's provides one option: use of the democratic process. The community—parents, students, teachers, school staff, and residents, together, can determine a content of character education through the democratic process—using the "ethical core of our social philosophy" to determine our core. However, before one embraces the concept of character education, a question seems appropriate: If schools and communities practiced social democracy as defined by reconstructionists, would character education be needed?

Angela Raffel (1996), a past chair of SER, also makes the connection between values and the tenet of democracy:

> Throughout American history, democracy has been considered a value. To be a reconstructionist means that we must uphold the tenet of democracy.

Along with establishing community values, reconstructionists believe that individuals must determine clarity in their value systems. Raffel (1990) refers to the pioneer work of Louis E. Raths in *Values and Teaching* (1966), in which Raths provides a seven-step process to determine if what one professes as a value actually is a value. The professed value must be:

1. Chosen freely;

2. Chosen from among alternatives;
3. Chosen after due reflection;
4. Affirmed publicly;
5. Prized and cherished;
6. Acted on;
7. Acted on repeatedly. (pp. 32-33)

Raths' seven-step process reflects Educational Reconstruction philosophy: there is reference to both thought and action, with emphasis upon action to determine if the value is "true."

Reconstructionists believe philosophy should serve as a guide to social action. It is this emphasis upon action, guided by thought and values, which is at the heart of Educational Reconstruction and the subject for the next section.

> **Action in the classroom:** Students and I identify recent significant events in our class, either individual or group. We then identify the value(s) upon which each episode is based, noting the values that are the foundation of action.

Action

The holistic nature of Educational Reconstruction is evident in its emphasis on linking thought with action, theory with practice. The importance of action is at the heart of a number of tenets in reconstruction as is evident in previous sections in this chapter which focused on action numerous times. For example, in the discussion on means and ends, action becomes a necessary component, for means become the action toward achievement of ends. In the discussion on truth and tested thought, action is viewed as the method of determining the validity of thought, as the method to recognize truth.

Reconstructionists believe that action can clarify, change, and increase knowledge and that there is often an ethical rationale for moving to action. Ozman referred to a painting on the third floor of the New York City Public Library as an indication of the ethical basis for putting ideas into action:

> It shows some monks busily working on their Bibles safe inside the monastery, while outside knights are burning down houses and cutting off the noses of the slower taxpayers. The monks saw no

need to utilize what knowledge they had for the improvement of [humanity] in *this* world; and one wonders, of course, what possible improvement it might make in the next. It is true that action without thought leads to detrimental ends, but its opposite, thought without action, is no more defensible. (p. 144)

The type of action associated with reconstruction is often labeled "social action." Conrad, in *Global Images of Peace and Education*, referred to Brameld's interpretation by stating that Brameld "always argued that philosophers of education must act on their belief" (p. 269). The example Conrad used to support his point is Brameld's involvement in political struggles during the anti-communism years of McCarthy when Brameld "refused to be intimidated." The acting as the basis of beliefs moves those who accept reconstruction, whether educator or other, into active roles.

Stone (1987) asserts that those drawn to Educational Reconstruction are

Social activists—people who have a need for moral uses of knowledge. It's not enough just to have a skill, or just to know something. How can you use it? Knowledge is sterile; knowledge in and of itself is not enough.

Langsam (1987) echoes Stone's perspective:

You certainly would say that educational reconstruction is action oriented. We are doing something. We just don't think ideas; we act.

The activism which reconstructionists embrace leads toward the achievement of a final reconstructionist tenet: peace.

Action in the classroom: Students and I develop a list of social actions we could carry out for the school or community and then develop a plan for implementation, relating work of preceding sections including identification of values, process of means and ends, change and tested thought, working toward the future (utopia concept), the common people, and the individual and community. All of this is done within the context of achieving academic ends.

Peace

Peace is more than prevention of war as conceived by reconstructionsts. According to the editors of *Global Images of Peace and Education* (1987), "peace means *shalom* or human well-being which suggests transformation both at personal and societal levels" (Preface). According to Thomas (*Images,* 1987), "Shalom has to do with a security that is physical as well as spiritual" (p. 13). And as Thomas points out in the preceding chapter of this volume, peace is more than merely maintaining harmony.

The language of transformation and action has appeared throughout the text of this publication, and it is the process of transformation through action that reconstructionists believe is vital to the achievement of a local and global peace. Examples of action are alleviating hunger in our neighborhood and beyond, working for an economic order which narrows the gap between the rich and the poor, seeking ways to avoid oppressing those who are different, carrying out community healing through restorative justice.

Within the school structure, the reference to Mitchell in the first chapter serves as an example. Mitchell envisioned bringing about global peace and order through linking people together in voluntary worldwide networks. The common problems of humanity would be the basis of the school curriculum and students would study and seek to address problems they identified in their own communities and beyond.

The process of peace through activism places one in contact with others who act. The action orientation of reconstructionists is, in part, a cause for those who accept its tenets to become aware of the changes which human interaction produces. This continuing change, or evolution, creates an awareness that human society never remains the same. As a result, reconstructionists believe that the thought which guides the action in a changing society must likewise be flexible and open to change. The philosophy of Educational Reconstruction, in short, remains unfinished.

> **Action in the classroom:** Students and I revisit the process of action we utilize to resolve our conflicts through non-violence as a means to understand the process of peace.

Unfinished

Although philosophy is often referred to as a guide for human behavior, some philosophies are more akin to purveying dogma and dictating human behavior. Brameld (*Patterns,* 1950), for instance, referred to perennialism as a philosophy which vests "ultimate rulership in those who, by definition, cannot be contradicted because they are their own supreme authority" (p. 373). In contrast, reconstruction takes the concept of guiding as a tenet. As a result, the philosophy cannot be finalized, for it must remain open to new thought which may develop as a result of what is learned through human action.

Frances L. O'Neil (1987), a member of SER and a practicing psychologist, discusses the nature of Educational Reconstruction:

> I think what is exciting about Educational Reconstruction is its integrity. It changes from decade to decade, which is as it should be, because it's a very active and involving kind of notion. When you're talking about reconstruction, whether it be personal or social, you are talking about a set of societal needs or educational needs that have to be reassessed and worked through in a pragmatic, yet far-sighted way.

A key concept in O'Neil's statement is *reassessed.* Because reconstruction avoids absolutism and is continually trying to determine what is universal within a relativistic framework, there is a necessity for a continuing reassessment.

There is evidence that O'Neil's reference to the process of reassessing Educational Reconstruction is being done. Stanley, in *Curriculum for Utopia* (1992), contends that, "...it is evident that there has been a widespread incorporation by liberal and radical educators of many elements of reconstructionist curriculum theory" (p. 192). Near the end of the publication, Stanley refers to his "reconceptualized reconstructionism" with his focus on critical pedagogy which he contends incorporates "the purpose of social reconstruction" (pp. 220-221).

Like some other philosophic views, critical pedagogy includes a diversity of interests and views such as neo-Marxism, feminism, cultural studies, neopragmatism, postmodernism, poststructuralism, Critical Theory, and the new sociology. According to Stanley, "...critical pedagogy has begun to give attention to and extended the analysis of issues raised by the reconstructionists" (pp. 5-6). The links between Educational Reconstruction and critical pedagogy include such elements as the political nature of schooling, the role of teachers in transforming culture, attention to ethical issues including social democratic values, and the view of the school as a means to challenge the existing order. Michael W. Apple (1995) contends reconstruction thought is alive:

> Thus, the original impulse of social reconstructionism to connect schools to progressive social purposes is not dead. It has re-emerged not only at the level of theory, but at the level of practice. And it is here where positive signs—not only negative tendencies—can give us some reason for hope. (p. 25)

William H. Fisher (1996), professor of history and philosophy of education at the University of Montana and an honorary member of SER, also believes that there is a renewed interest in reconstructionist thinking:

> With the resurgence in very recent times of an interest in Pragmatism—witness the work of Richard Rorty, *et al.*—inevitably, this has led to a resurgence of interest in progressive education (or would a better term, now, be "neo-progessivism")....and inevitably also this has caused thoughtful scholars and educators to "dust off" their copies of the works of Ted Brameld, *et al.* So: A fair question is—have writers, scholars, teachers, such as Brameld lost their relevance in today's world? I, of course, think not!!

As reconstructionist thought developed after mid-century, Berkson (1950) appears to have articulated what remains a present-day perspective of how reconstructionists see the process of philosophy. According to Berkson, "A philosophy, though clearly formulated, need not be final for all times and places; nor need it be worked out beforehand in all detail" (p. 40). O'Neil states that reconstruction "is not a time-limited philosophy at all." Stone (1996) presents a challenge to his reconstructionist colleagues: "We need to frame our position in light of current and emerging social reality, not on the basis of the nineteenth or even the twentieth century mentalities." Benne (1995) also sees the need to continue a reconstructionist influence: "I believe we need a new social reconstructionist movement in American education with links to kindred education movements in other nations" (p. xxv).

The philosophy of Educational Reconstruction is not final for all times, although some basic concepts provide the foundation for thought. According to Berkson (1940), "The main pattern of values, the central line of conduct, the fundamental intellectual assumptions must be stated" (p. 40). This chapter on some tenets of reconstruction philosophy has attempted to do that. The aim has been to present the main pattern of reconstruction values, and to discuss the nature of conduct within such a framework of values based on fundamental intellectual assumptions.

> **Action in the classroom:** Students and I develop our individual lifelines (history) and each identifies what remains to be lived: the "unfinished business" of our lives.

Summary

The following is a summary, based on the tenets of Educational Reconstruction as discussed in this chapter:

A philosophy of Educational Reconstruction is a holistic perspective which seeks to transmit and transform culture through education in the context of a social and ethical democracy.

Educational Reconstruction's futuristic, utopian, (radical) and hopeful nature suggests that change is a fact and that humankind must take responsibility in directing change.

Change is viewed as necessary because of existing crises. However, change must be a result of tested thought put into action without violence through the interdependence of means and ends.

Action guided by Educational Reconstruction thought seeks to benefit the individual and the community to achieve peace locally and globally.

Educational Reconstruction is on-going.

Notes

1. Theodore Brameld began writing while Mumford developed and shared his view of the need for a different way of thinking, using the language of transformation in *The Transformation of Man*. Mumford's influence is evident in Brameld's many references and in the language of reconstruction which relies on the language and theme of transformation.

    Robert Jay Lifton (1987) explained a view of transformation: "[It] must connect with the past while going beyond mere survival of that past in the creation of new forms and modes. The process is both psychological and historical, and at the same time prominently aesthetic" (p. 69). Other reconstructionists continue to utilize the language and idea of transformation. For example, Gertrude F. Langsam (1987), charter member of the Society for Educational Reconstruction, stated, "As we struggle to build this better world, we know that individual growth is central and that is what we mean by the goal self-transformation. At the same time, we must be aware of our responsibilities toward the larger needs of humanity and look toward the goal of social-transformation" (p. 40). Another example is David R. Conrad, (1976), in his title *Education for Transformation: Implications in Lewis Mumford's Ecohumanism*.

    A final example is the Society for Educational Reconstruction (SER) which cites one of its four concepts or goals as "self-transformation."

    Brameld, like Mumford, saw the need for a transformation, the need for a vision with unity as a theme: unity in thought and unity in action. It became Brameld's mission to create this vision, transformation, and new way of thinking.

2. Harold Rugg's "school-centered community" seems worthy of special attention since it would be easy to dismiss it as "community-centered school." Although both concepts indicate a strong relationship between school and society, and both concepts are acceptable in the reconstructionist view, there is a difference.

    Rugg's concept of "school-centered community" seems truer to the reconstructionist position since it is more inclusive, viewing education and transformation anywhere. Rugg reported that the concept was actually suggested to him by Clare Soper, secretary of the New Education Fellowship in London. Rugg (1931) suggested that the concept should be the ideal toward which efforts be expended. He defined the school-centered community as "a society in which home, government, industries, trade, farms, organizations, all the social agencies, will perceive their educational as well as their maintenance functions" (p. 288). He further explained the concept as a coordinated system of both adult and child education touching all phases of community life through a "unified educational system integrating all the social agencies of the community, at every age-level from infancy to old age" (p. 289).

Rugg's description appears to describe Brameld's visual model of education and culture, presented earlier in the discussion, where education touches all aspects directly.

In the preceding chapter, Mitchell's reference to the campus of the school being coterminous with the community is consistent with the views of Rugg and Raup.

3. Anthropotherapy is a concept developed by Brameld. According to Frank Stone, it is a process of making it possible for people to interact; a process where people are brought in contact with those they would not normally see. One can sense the reconstructionist view of democracy in Stone's idea—participation of all citizens, not just a representational structure. It is an inclusive process for directing change.

In *The Climactic Decades,* Brameld defined anthropotherapy as "the theory and practice of descriptive and prescriptive human roles. It provides analyses particularly of conflictive and cooperative situations and makes characterizing value judgments in the light of such analyses" (p. 130).

Greater clarity of the concept appeared in his later collaborative work with Matsuyama where they explained it as "a provocative way of symbolizing an old idea—namely, that cultural learning (especially in an anthropological sense) is much more than learning *about* living cultures. It connotes equally participating, observing, and becoming involved in the problems and disturbances of living cultures. Somewhat analogously with psychotherapy, anthropotherapy thus becomes an application of the sciences of human behavior to indirect and direct action toward character change—in this case, above all, socio-cultural change" (p. 176).

In comparing the three references cited, participation and inclusivity toward cultural change appear to be common ideas in Brameld's concept of anthropotherapy.

References

Apple, Michael W. (1995). Is Social Transformation Always Progressive? In Michael E. James, ed., *Social Reconstruction Through Education.* Norwood, NJ: Ablex Publishing Corporation.

Beard, Charles A., ed. (1932). *America Faces the Future.* Boston and New York: Houghton Mifflin Company.

Beard, Charles A. (1932). *A Charter for the Social Sciences in the Schools.* Report of the Commission on the Social Studies, Part I. New York: Charles Scribner's Sons.

Beard, Charles A. (1934). *The Nature of the Social Sciences in Relation to Objectives of Instruction.* Report of the Commission on the Social Studies Part VII. New York: Charles Scribner's Sons.

Bellamy, Edward. (1946). *Looking Backward.* Cleveland, OH: The World Publishing Co.

Benne, Kenneth D. (1943). *A Conception of Authority: An Introductory Study.* New York: Teachers College, Columbia University.

Benne, Kenneth D. (1956). The Content of a Contemporary Philosophy of Education. *Harvard Educational Review,* XXVI No. 2, 127-30.

Benne, Kenneth D. (1995). Prologue: Social Reconstructionism Remembered. In Michael E. James, ed., *Social Reconstruction Through Education.* Norwood, NJ: Ablex Publishing Corporation.

Berkson, I.B. (1940). *Preface to an Educational Philosophy.* New York: Columbia University Press.

Berkson, I.B. (1943). *Education Faces the Future: An Appraisal of Contemporary Movements in Education.* New York: Harper & Brothers.

Berkson, I.B. (1958).*The Ideal and the Community: A Philosophy of Education.* New York: Harper & Brothers.

Bode, Boyd H. (1927). *Modern Educational Theories.* New York: The Macmillan Company.

Bode, Boyd H. (1933). The Confusion in Present-Day Education. In William Heard Kilpatrick, ed., *The Educational Frontier.* New York: The Century Company.

Bode, Boyd H. (1938). *Progressive Education at the Crossroads.* New York and Chicago: Newson & Company.

Boyer, William. (1978). Forward. In Theodore Brameld & Midori Matsuyama, *Tourism and Cultural Learning: Two Controversial Case Studies in Educational Anthropology.* University Press of America, division of: Washington, DC: R.F. Publishing, Inc.

Brameld, Theodore. (1933). *A Philosophical Approach to Communism.* Chicago, IL: University of Chicago Press.

Brameld, Theodore. (1945). *Design for America: An Educational Exploration of the Future of Democracy.* New York: Hinds, Hayden & Eldredge.

Brameld, Theodore. (1950). *Ends and Means in Education: A Midcentury Appraisal.* New York: Harper & Brothers.

Brameld, Theodore. (1950). *Patterns of Educational Philosophy: A Democratic Interpretation.* New York: World Book Co.

Brameld, Theodore. (1955). *Philosophies of Education in Cultural Perspective.* New York: Dryden Press.

Brameld, Theodore. (1956). Education for What? *The Education Digest*, 21, 20-33.

Brameld, Theodore. (1956). *Toward a Reconstructed Philosophy of Education*. New York: Dryden Press.

Brameld, Theodore. (1957). *Cultural Foundations of Education: An Interdisciplinary Exploration*. New York: Harper & Brothers.

Brameld, Theodore. (1959). Imperatives for a Reconstructed Philosophy of Education. *School and Society*, 87, 18-20.

Brameld, Theodore. (1964). Values: Education's Most Neglected Problem. In Stanley Elam & Theodore Brameld, eds., *Values in American Education*. Bloomington, IN: Phi Delta Kappa, Inc., 1964.

Brameld, Theodore. (1965). *Education as Power*. New York: Holt, Rinehart, & Winston.

Brameld, Theodore. (1965). *Education for the Emerging Age: Newer Ends and Stronger Means*. New York: Harper & Row.

Brameld, Theodore. (1965). *The Use of Explosive Ideas in Education, Culture, Class, and Evolution*. Pittsburgh, PA: University of Pittsburgh Press.

Brameld, Theodore. (1966). Reconstructionist Theory: Some Recent Critiques Considered in Perspective. *Educational Theory*, 15-16, 333-43.

Brameld, Theodore. (1968). *Japan: Culture, Education, and Change in Two Communities*. New York: Holt, Rinehart & Winston.

Brameld, Theodore. (1970). *The Climactic Decade: Mandate to Education*. New York: Praeger Publishers.

Brameld, Theodore. (1973). Self-fulfilling Prophecy as an Educational Perspective. In Nobuo Shimahara, ed., *Educational Reconstruction: Promise and Challenge*. Columbus, OH: Charles E. Merrill Publishing.

Brameld, Theodore. (1977). Reconstructionism as Radical Philosophy of Education: A Reappraisal. *The Educational Forum*, XLII, 67-76.

Brameld, Theodore. (n.d.). *The Teacher as World Citizen*. Kappa Delta Pi Press.

Brameld, Theodore, & Midori Matsuyama. (1978). *Tourism as Cultural Learning*. University Press of America, division of: Washington, D.C: R.F. Publishing, Inc.

Brameld, Midori Matsuyama. See Matsuyama, Midori.

Burns, Hobert W. (1965). Brameld's Reconstructionism Reviewed. *Phi Delta Kappan*, 47, 147-50.

Bussler, Darrol. (1994). The Democratic Class. *Teacher Education Quarterly*. Vol 21. No. 4, 23-46.

Chambliss, J.J. (1988). Reconstructionism Remembered: Theodore Brameld, 1904-1987. *Educational Theory*, 38, 379-388.

Childs, John L. (1959). John Dewey and American Education. *Teachers College Record*, 61, 128-33.

Conrad, David R. (1976). *Education for Transformation: Implications in Lewis Mumford's Ecohumanism.* Palm Springs, CA: An ETC Publication.

Conrad, David R. (1987). University of Vermont, Burlington. Telephone interview conducted by Darrol Bussler from South St. Paul, MN on October 27.

Conrad, David R. (1987). Brameld as Visionary Educator. In Nobuo Shimahara, ed., *Educational Reconstruction: Promise and Challenge.* Columbus, OH: Charles E. Merrill Publishing Co.

Counts, George S. (1930). *The American Road to Culture: A Social Interpretation of Education in the United States.* New York: The John Day Company.

Counts, George S. (1932). *Dare the School Build a New Social Order?* New York: The John Day Company.

Counts, George S. (1938). *The Prospects of American Democracy.* New York: The John Day Company.

Counts, George S. (1962). *Education and the Foundations of Human Freedom.* Pittsburgh, PA: University of Pittsburgh Press.

Dewey, John. (1897). *My Pedagogic Creed.* In Lawrence A. Cremin ed., (1959), *Dewey on Education.* With Introduction and Notes by Martin S. Dworkin. Classics in Education Series, No. 3. New York: Teachers College, Columbia University.

Dewey, John. (1900). *The School and Society.* New York: McClure, Phillips & Company.

Dewey, John. (1916). *Democracy and Education: An Introduction to the Philosophy of Education.* New York: The MacMillan Company.

Dewey, John. (1920). *Reconstruction in Philosophy.* New York: Henry Holt & Company.

Dewey, John & John L. Childs. (1933). The Social-Economic Situation and Education. In William H. Kilpatrick, ed., *The Educational Frontier.* New York, London: The Century Co.

Dewey, John & John L. Childs. (1933). The Underlying Philosophy of Education. In William H. Kilpatrick, ed., *The Educational Frontier.* New York, London: The Century Co.

Fisher, William H. (1996). University of Montana, Missoula. Letter to Darrol Bussler, Chair of SER Executive Board, dated June 10.

Frankena, William K. (1965). *Three Historical Philosophies of Education: Aristotle, Kant, Dewey.* Chicago, IL: Scott, Foresman & Company.

Gutek, Gerald L. (1989). The Contributions of George S. Counts. Paper presented at the American Educational Studies Association Conference, Chicago, IL.

Gutek, Gerald L. (1970). *The Educational Theory of George S. Counts.* Columbus, OH: Ohio State University Press.

Hullfish, H. Gordon & V.T. Thayer. (1933). The School: Its Task and Its Administration—I. In William H. Kilpatrick ed., *The Educational Frontier*. New York, London: The Century Co.

James, Michael E., ed. (1995). *Social Reconstruction Through Education— The Philosophy, History, and Curricula of a Radical Ideal*. Norwood, NJ: Ablex Publishing Corporation.

James, Michael E. (1995). Southern Progressivism and the Great Depression. In Michael E. James, ed., *Social Reconstruction Through Education— The Philosophy, History, and Curricula of a Radical Ideal*. Norwood, NJ: Ablex Publishing Corporation.

Kandel, I.L. (1930). *Essays in Comparative Education*. New York: Teachers College, Columbia University.

Kandel, I.L. (1933). Can the School Build a New Social Order? *The Kadelpian Review*, XII, 143-53.

Kandel, I.L. (1933). Education and Social Disorder. *Teachers College Record* XXXIV, 359-67.

Kandel, I.L. (1957). *American Education in the Twentieth Century*. Cambridge, MA: Harvard University Press.

Kant, Immanuel. (1904). In Edward Franklin Bucher, ed., *The Educational Theory of Immanuel Kant*. Lippincott Educational Series, Martin G. Brumbaugh, ed. Vol. IV. Philadelphia, PA: J.B. Lippincott Company.

Kant, Immanuel. (1930). *Lectures on Ethics*. Translated by Louis Infield. London: Methuen & Co., Ltd.

Kilpatrick, William Heard. (1926). *Education for a Changing Civilization*. New York: The Macmillan Company.

Kilpatrick, William Heard. (1931). *A Reconstructed Theory of The Educative Process*. New York: Teachers College, Columbia University.

Kilpatrick, William Heard. (1932). *Education and the Social Crisis: A Proposed Program*. New York: Liveright, Inc.

Kilpatrick, William Heard, ed. (1933). *The Educational Frontier*. New York: The Century Co.

Kilpatrick, William Heard. (1939). The Promise of Education. *The New Republic*. November.

Kilpatrick, William Heard. (1940). *Group Education for a Democracy*. New York: Association Press.

Kilpatrick, William Heard. (1941). *Selfhood and Civilization: A Study of the Self-Other Process*. New York: The Macmillan Company.

Kneller, George F. (1967). The Angels and Demons of Theodore Brameld. *Educational Theory*, 17-18, 73-5.

Kropotkin, P. (1902). *Mutual Aid: A Factor of Evolution*. London: William Heinemann. Fourth Impression, April, 1910.

Langsam, Gertrude F. (1987). Adelphi University. Telephone interview conducted by Darrol Bussler from South St. Paul, Minnesota on Nov. 4.

Langsam, Gertrude F. (1987). Toward a New Human Community: Using the Arts in Teacher Education. In Nobuo Shimahara, ed., *Educational Reconstruction: Promise and Challenge.* Columbus, OH: Charles E. Merrill Publishing Co.

Laski, Harold J. (1936). A New Education for a New America. *The New Republic,* 87, 342-345.

Laski, Harold J. (1940). *The Rights of Man.* London: Macmillan & Co., Ltd.

Laski, Harold J. (1948).*The American Democracy: A Commentary and Interpretation.* New York: The Viking Press.

Lifton, Robert J. (1987). A Psychocultural Perspective. In Nobuo Shimahara, ed., *Educational Reconstruction.* Columbus, OH: Charles E. Merrill Publishing Company.

Mannheim, Karl. (1941). *Man and Society in an Age of Reconstruction.* New York: Harcourt, Brace & Company.

Matsuyama (Brameld), Midori. (1987). Durham, NC. Interviews conducted by Darrol Bussler on September 15 and 16.

Mead, George. (1934). *Mind, Self & Society: From the Standpoint of a Social Behaviorist.* Chicago, IL: The University of Chicago Press.

Meiklejohn, Alexander. (1942). *Education Between Two Worlds.* New York: Harper & Brothers.

Mumford, Lewis. (1956). *The Transformations of Man.* World Perspectives (Series), Ruth Nanda Anshen, ed., vol. seven. New York: Harper & Brothers.

O'Neil, Francis L. (1987). Tunxis Community College, Farmington, CT. Telephone interview conducted by Darrol Bussler from South St. Paul, MN on November 11.

Nash, Paul. (1973). Towards a Radical View of Authority Relationships in Education. In Nobuo Shimahara, ed., *Educational Reconstruction: Promise and Challenge.* Columbus, OH: Charles E. Merrill Publishing Company.

Nash, Paul. (1989). Progressive Agenda for the 1990s. Keynote address to the Society for Educational Reconstruction: Brameld Symposium. University of Bridgeport, Bridgeport, CT on March 19.

Ozman, Howard. (1973). A Philosophical Perspective. In Nobuo Shimahara, ed., *Educational Reconstruction: Promise and Challenge.* Columbus, OH: Charles E. Merrill Publishing Company.

Raffel, Angela. The Relationship Between the Personal Values of Junior High and High School Teachers and Their Educational Philosophies. Unpublished Ph.D. Dissertation. University of Bridgeport, Bridgeport, CT August, 1990.

Raffel, Angela. (1996). Valley Cottage, NY. Telephone interview conducted by Darrol Bussler from South St. Paul, MN on June 11.

Raup, Bruce. (1936). *Education and Organized Interests in America.* New York: G.P. Putnam's Sons.

Raup, Bruce, George E. Axtell, Kenneth D. Benne, and B. Othanel Smith. (1950). The *Improvement of Practical Intelligence*. New York: Harper & Brothers.

Report of the Commission on the Social Studies. (1934). *Conclusions and Recommendations of the Commission*. New York: Charles Scribner's Sons.

Rugg, Harold. (1931). *Culture and Education in America*. New York: Harcourt, Brace & Company.

Rugg, Harold. (1933). *The Great Technology: Social Chaos and the Public Mind*. New York: The John Day Company.

Rugg, Harold. (1933). *Social Reconstruction: Study Guide for Group and Class Discussion*. New York: The John Day Company.

Rugg, Harold. (1957). Schools of Creative Life...an Unfinished Business in Education. *The National Elementary Principal*. XXXVI, 12-15.

Semel, Susan F. (1995). Female Founders and the Progressive Paradox. In Michael E. James, ed., *Social Reconstruction Through Education*. Norwood, NJ: Ablex Publishing Corporation.

Shimahara, Nobuo, ed. (1973). *Educational Reconstruction: Promise and Challenge*. Columbus, OH: Charles E. Merrill Publishing Co.

Shimahara, Nobuo. (1973). Introduction: Toward a Transformative Psychocultural Orientation. In Nobuo Shimahara, ed., *Educational Reconstruction: Promise and Challenge*. Columbus, OH: Charles E. Merrill Publishing Co.

Shimahara, Nobuo. (1987). Rutgers University, Princeton Junction, NY. Telephone interview conducted by Darrol Bussler from South St. Paul, MN on November 22.

Smith, Jay M. (1987). Ser [sic] An Organization Committed to Global Peace. In T.M. Thomas, David R. Conrad, & Gertrude F. Langsam, eds., *Global Images of Peace and Education: Transforming the War System*. Ann Arbor, MI: Prakken Publications, Inc..

Smith, T.V. (1927). *The American Philosophy of Equality*. Chicago, IL: The University of Chicago Press.

Smith, T.V. (1942). *Discipline for Democracy*. Chapel Hill, NC: University of North Carolina Press.

Smith, T.V. & Eduard C. Lindeman. (1926). *The Democratic Way of Life*. New York: The New American Library.

Smith, T.V., & Robert J. Taft. (1939). *Foundations of Democracy*. New York: Alfred A. Knopf.

Society for Educational Reconstruction. (1968). Statement of Purpose. Nobuo Shimahara, Chair.

Society for Educational Reconstruction. *SER in Action!* Newsletter.

Stanley, William B. (1992). *Curriculum for Utopia*. Albany, NY: State University of New York Press.

Stanley, William O. & Kenneth D. Benne. (1995). Social Reconstructionism for 21st-century Educators. In Michael E. James ed., *Social Reconstruction Through Education—The Philosophy, History, and Curricula of a Radical Ideal.* Norwood, NJ: Ablex Publishing Corporation.

Stone, Frank A. (1987). University of Connecticut, Storrs, CT. Telephone interviews conducted by Darrol Bussler from South St. Paul, MN on September 3 and 30.

Stone, Frank A. (1996). Letters to Darrol Bussler dated June 12 and June 10.

Thomas, T.M. & John B. Chethimattam. (1974). *Images of Man.* Bangalore, India: Dharmaram Publications.

Thomas, T.M. (1987). University of Bridgeport, Bridgeport, CT. Telephone interview conducted by Darrol Bussler from South St. Paul, MN on November 16.

Thomas, T.M. (1987). Introduction: From a Warring World to a Peaceful Global Order. In T.M. Thomas, David R. Conrad, & Gertrude F. Langsam, eds., *Global Images of Peace and Education: Transforming the War System.* Ann Arbor, MN: Prakken Publications, Inc.

Thomas, T.M. (1989). University of Bridgeport, Bridgeport, CT. Interview conducted by Darrol Bussler on March 18.

Thomas, T.M., David R. Conrad, & Gertrude F. Langsam, eds. (1987). *Global Images of Peace and Education: Transforming the War System.* Ann Arbor, MI: Prakken Publications, Inc.

Woolman, David. C. (1987). World Order for Peace, Philosophical Approaches of Brameld and Galtung. In T.M. Thomas, David R. Conrad, & Gertrude F. Langsam, eds., *Global Images of Peace and Education: Transforming the War System.* Ann Arbor, MI: Prakken Publications, Inc.

Yarbrough, Dean. (1996). Memorial Day address at Town Hall, Sudbury, MA on May 14.

Chapter 4

EDUCATIONAL RECONSTRUCTION IN THE FUTURE

By Frances L. O'Neil

Introduction

According to the projections of the United States Census Bureau (1991), the face of American society will be radically altered within the next fifty years. When one considers the fact that in the first U.S. Census conducted in 1790, the 3.9 million people were almost invariably white and of European heritage, the predictions are even more dramatic. (Apparently Native Americans were awarded the status of non-persons at the time, because they were not counted.) With the exception of the Africans brought to America as slaves, that pattern of immigration from Europe continued without variation for nearly two centuries. However, since the 1980s, four out of five immigrants have entered the United States from Asia, Latin America, and the Caribbean, and in all likelihood that distribution will continue. If the present projections are correct, the 71 percent white Americans registered in the 1990 census will decline to 53 percent by 2050. While the percentage of African Americans, Asian Americans, and Native Americans will rise slightly by that year, the demographic projections of the Urban Institute indicate that the present figure of 9 percent Hispanic Americans will rise to 25 percent within the next century.

In an article in *American Demographics*, Thomas G. Exter (1993) has claimed that these shifts will have particular impact in the economic sphere:

> As non-Hispanic whites age, they will be increasingly dependent on the productivity of black, Hispanic, and Asian workers. More than half of the nation's new workers between 1990 and 2005 will be minorities, according to the Bureau of Labor Statistics. Increasingly, the fortunes of America's minorities will affect the well-being of the majority. (p.59)

American society is changing in other ways. The number of older Americans is increasing steadily, as well as the awareness of persons with disabilities. The latest figures reveal that approximately 15 percent of our population experiences a disability which restricts their daily activities. Those who teach college students do not need to be informed that our college population has undergone a radical shift as well. It was not long ago that incoming first-year students were white, pre-dominantly male, and high school graduates. Now, more than half of college students are female, and 43 percent are 25 and older.

This diversity of population will most certainly have an impact on the subject matter of research. Historically, the dominant culture has influenced the values, categories, and terms of the academic enterprise. Within the past several decades, however, we have come to realize that the very way in which data is gathered inescapably reflects the attitudes of the groups engaged in the research. How often, we might ask ourselves, have the views of women, children, and the elderly been included in the historical and sociological research of the past. In 1976, Jean Baker Miller's *Toward a New Psychology of Women* challenged prevailing psychological theories, while Carol Gilligan (1982) gathered empirical data that reflected fundamental differences in the development of men and women. Their pioneering efforts demonstrated that a body of information emerges, which is different in kind, when women are included in such studies, both as informants and as researchers.

Three important themes run through Miller's work, and though she focused on the role of women, her findings have many implications for other minority groups. It is her contention that we cannot have meaningful discourse about the characteristics of people and societies apart from their cultural context. In a system in which women have less power, they become adept at balancing relationships that are "unequal and essentially nonmutual." In this one-down situation people adapt in ways that are often misunderstood by the dominant group and so their disempowered status is perpetuated.

Another central theme in women's lives is the forging and maintenance of cooperative relationships rather than an overweening emphasis on independence, autonomy, and, by extension, competition. Miller's third premise states that when cooperation is viewed as a strength rather than a weakness, it can lead into new pathways of social behavior that have wide-reaching implications. For example, empowering connotes "fostering the growth of others" as opposed to "power over others"(p. 117).

How Do We Know

In *Women's Ways of Knowing* (1986) Belenky, Clinchy, Goldberger, and Tarule interviewed "ordinary women living ordinary lives"(p. 4). The process of drawing together this material focused a glaring spotlight on the fact that common concepts of knowledge and truth have been shaped throughout history by a white, male-dominated culture. In giving form to their visions, men have constructed theories which have now become gospel for both men and women. The four authors discuss powerful alternative ways of knowing: listening, received knowledge, subjective knowledge, procedural knowledge, and finally, constructed knowledge. They are convinced that:

> It is in the process of sorting out the pieces of the self and of searching for a unique and authentic voice that women come to the basic insights of constructivist thought: "All knowledge is constructed" and "the knower is an intimate part of the known." (p. 137)

As women become more aware that social reality has been constructed for them and begin to engage in the powerful process of forging their own view of the world, on what support systems can they depend? The Judeo-Christian traditions that so permeate the ethical standards of Western culture have certainly not provided leadership on this matter. Elizabeth Cady Stanton (1888) may have overstated the case a bit when she declared,

> ...a consideration of women's position shows that she is not

indebted to any form of religion for one step of progress or one new liberty; on the contrary, it has been through the perversion of her religious sentiments that she has been so long held in a condition of slavery. (Quoted in Oakley, 1972, p. 112)

But few of us would disagree with her thesis that two thousand years of this mode of thought and action have failed to bring about the necessary social and conceptual changes.

Should women look, then, to rational thinking and the scientific method to produce evidence that would further their inclusion in the gathering and interpretation of data and the creation of theory. There seems little justification for that approach, either. Many feminists feel that the cult of objectivity has a distinctly masculine bias, with its emphasis on manipulation, control, and distance from the object. Because rationality has been regarded as infallible, women and the modes of thought most utilized by women have had little impact on the direction of modern society.

Many feminists, like pragmatists and postmodernists, reject the notion that knowledge can be grounded in an antecedent set of premises. Casting doubt on one of science's most prominent claims, some authors have asserted that:

> Since it is impossible to build an argument or interpret an event without a purpose or perspective, objectivity becomes a myth. (Belenky, *et al.*, 1986, p. 137)

This constructivist view was very ably expressed by Gregory Bateson in *Steps to an Ecology of Mind* (1972) and in all of Paul Watzlawick's books. In an interview (1995), Watzlawick commented on the fact that each individual has the delusion that the way she sees things is the way they really are. Of the real reality, we can only know what it is not. We know it only through the breakdown of our construction. Throughout his book *How Real is Real* (1976), he has demonstrated how "assumptions, beliefs, premises, superstitions, hopes and the like, may become more real than reality" (p. 43), creating a web of delusions. Not only are the contents of our "invented reality" idiosyncratic, but the very way in which we gather data to form our world view is extremely variable, as well. As the constructivist Ernst von Glasersfeld (1984) has stated,

> What we experience, cognize, and come to know is necessarily built up of our own building blocks and can be explained in no other way

124

than in terms of our ways and means of building... Whatever we
choose as building blocks become our limiting constraints, but we
experience these constraints from the inside. (p. 32)

While the implications of this theory may give us all a bit of vertigo,
its hypotheses can be profoundly liberating for women and other
minorities, because it suggests that we are at risk when we accept
"knowledge" without examining it in its social and political context.
For example, the meaning of the words you are now reading reflects
a reality which has been formed through the author's subjective
experience, and you are interpreting her representation through your
own private lens. Intellectual inquiry, then, becomes a sociology of
knowledge.

The Women
of the Society for Educational Reconstruction

Despite the fact that the Society for Educational Reconstruction
(SER) is profoundly committed to strengthening the educational and
social rights of the individual, there has been a notable lack of research
and social action concerning the rights of women—and when there
has been activity, it was due to the vision of several enlightened men.
As the members look to the future, this imbalance needs to be
corrected. If we survey the literature of SER since the 1960s, we can
find many images of women in the search for peace and in the
employment of the arts as an agent for transforming society, but there
has been very little critical examination of the masculine biases that
are attached to the very goals that we pursue. As Mary Daly (1974)
has said, "The very naming of the ends and purposes has always
resided with men and has left many highly intelligent women stam-
mering and without an adequate voice"(p. 35). I have attempted to
offer five women, long-term members of SER, that "voice" by asking
them why so few of us have ever written or spoken on feminist issues.

Gertrude F. Langsam is a charter member of the Society, and, in
all likelihood, she and her husband, Henry, have been associated with
Theordore Brameld and the philosophy of Educational Reconstruction longer than any other members. In an interview, she vividly
described her experiences in applying for work during the Great
Depression. The focus on economic survival was so imperative at that
time that many other social issues became secondary. She was one of

the first women in New York City to edit a trade newspaper, and it was her contention that if you did your job well and met the requirements of your employer, you would be successful, whether you were a man or woman. Another major problem was the prejudice shown toward Jewish workers. She recalls that one time she was hired for an interesting position, but when she discovered that the owners had changed their names so that they would fit the Anglo-Saxon image, she could not remain in that environment. It is her sense that the women of her generation were so involved in issues of economic security and prejudicial treatment that the timing was not right for the type of study and action that needs to be done today.

Annamma Thomas is Indian-born and has been a member of the Society for over twenty-five years. As the wife of one of our co-authors and an educator in her own right, she came to know Brameld and his work firsthand. She feels that the Society has always dealt with feminist issues adequately. She recalls that an SER conference was held in 1991 called, "Women on the Move," at which members such as Midori Matsuyama and David Conrad spoke. She states that women have always been represented on panels and that she, herself, spoke on literacy at a recent American Educational Studies Association conference. She has great hope and sees much progress for women worldwide. "The 1996 Olympics offers a good example," she says, "of women's ability to forge ahead and to compete."

Angela Raffel is a past president of SER. She has demonstrated an indomitable spirit as she has attempted to follow through on the goals of the Society. Although she has written often and well, she states that she did not pursue women's issues specifically because she tended to be influenced by the topics outlined by the men in the organization. She calls this diffidence "ridiculous" now, but she can understand how it happened because she continues to have such respect for their expertise.

As the daughter of a very independent mother, Angela claims that she never felt restricted as a woman until later in her career. She describes her attendance at a professional meeting at which she offered a suggestion that was completely ignored. Later, when the same idea was put forth by a male committee member, it was accepted enthusiastically. This was but one example of many instances of discrimination.

Angela was in her middle years when she entered a Ph.D.

program. It was quite apparent to her and the other women in her age group that certain professors went out of their way to put stumbling blocks in their path. How much of this prejudice against them related to their gender and how much to ageism was difficult to determine, but Dr. Raffel is under no illusion about academia being free of sexism.

Midori Matsuyama Kiso is our "Japanese connection." She is the widow of Theodore Brameld and was present at the founding of the Society in 1967. She is the only one of the five of us who has spoken specifically on the status of women, often comparing the lifestyles of Japanese women to women in America. She is loathe to say that the work of SER authors over the past thirty years has "failed" to address feminist issues because "the philosophy of Educational Reconstruction has been influencing the rise and continuation of feminist controversies through the ideas, for example, of social-self-realization and anthropotherapy." Yet she does admit that no "hard" research evidence or straightforward writings on women's issues has yet appeared in SER-related work and "it's high time it did." She hopes that through the process of social-self-realization, women may start to understand their place in the cultural milieu which may emphasize a "women's culture" distinct from the "culture of males." Rather than being dichotomized, however, these cultures should eventually blend to create a coherent whole.

In recounting my own experience, I must say that I was initially drawn to SER because of the breadth of its vision and the attempts of its members to express that ideal in concrete form. As we wrote and worked on ecological issues, peace studies, world education, and racial equality, it seemed to me at the time that feminist issues were part of a broader agenda and, as such, were not excluded. In the 1970s, when it came time to select my dissertation topic, I chose to research the psychological and educational techniques of the masters of East Asia, hoping that this would expand my intercultural understanding and deepen and enrich my students' experience as well. Ted Brameld was disappointed. Although he (1977) had written about Zen Buddhism as "one of the perspectives on the human condition that contributes importantly to the search for culturological convergence"(p. 74), his response to my announcement was "I had hoped you'd research some aspect of sexism and education." As I look back on that time, it seems to me that I was so overwhelmed as a struggling single mother of three young sons that the social issues were much too close to home for me to study them with any degree of objectivity. But my decision was certainly not due to any barriers placed in my way by the men involved in Educational Reconstruction. Not only Brameld, but my past advisor and present co-author, Frank Stone, would have welcomed such a pursuit.

Interestingly enough, the men in SER have been more directly involved in feminist research. In his *Peoples of Connecticut* series, Stone examined the various roles of African-American women, and in 1995 he served as major advisor to Elizabeth Ann Flesor as she wrote a fine master's thesis entitled "Current Feminist Theory Applied to Practices at a University-Based Women's Center." Both in his articles and in his presentations, Conrad, a professor at the University of Vermont, has explored the impact of women artists on people's social consciousness. Without exception, the men and women of SER who work at the college and university levels have been extremely supportive of women students, and it would not be difficult to demonstrate the cascade effect of their commitment over the past thirty years.

This could serve as a lesson for those who find themselves in a minority position and seemingly without a voice, for they should be aware that there are times when "the fault is not in the stars, but in ourselves." If we persist in our convictions, we may find as many supporters as adversaries in our search for equality and justice. Perhaps, I still may be able to right this imbalance in my own professional development.

What Now?

As Brameld (1974) reviewed his long career, he had this to say,

During much of my education from nursery school to university graduation and even during my subsequent twenty-six years as a teacher, I have had virtually to unlearn too much of what was originally learned, or rather was literally conditioned to learn. (p. 67)

There is an inherent sadness in this statement, implying as it does that so much time was wasted on the acquisition of useless knowledge which would later require more time and energy to expunge. We have come to uneasy terms with the fact that information becomes obsolescent literally overnight, but there is the real possibility that some of our most cherished values and even the foundations of our knowledge will be overturned as well. What skills can we bring to bear on such complex issues as physician-assisted suicide and genetic manipulation, for example? Brameld spoke of "participation in communicating, planning, agreeing, and acting":

> If people...cannot learn by such participation as to how to confront each other, how to engage in creative dialogue, how to resolve conflicts, how to respect disagreements, how to translate general commonalities into specific actions of testable workability, then I should say that the hope of world order as a human order is very bleak indeed. (p. 67)

Brameld (1972), in his article "Education as Self-Fulfilling Prophecy," and more recently Neil Postman (1995) in *The End of Education* ask about the myths that give meaning and purpose to our lives. Myths are not mere fabrications, but rather the expression of deeply felt needs and desires. Postman constructs five tales relating to common themes which direct our lives. One he calls "The Word Weavers/The World Makers" in which he relates several instances where teachers, by making chance comments, have set students on paths that would determine their future course. It is through images and the use of language that we create the world. "We see the world as it permits us to see it" (p. 83).

For those of us who belong to segments of society that historically have been underrepresented and sometimes misrepresented, we may find that we do not have to look far for ways of correcting society's faulty images—first in our own minds and then in the views of others. From our Greek and Roman heritage, we are familiar with Homer's beautiful Helen of Troy and Virgil's lonely and patient Dido, but they are anemic characters, poorly developed and unsuited to the rigors of modern life. A far better image for the tasks that confront us is that of Queen Medb (Mayv), so realistically presented in the Irish prose epic, *Tain Bo Cuailnge*. The manuscript dates to the eighth century, but it is based on an oral tradition that may well go back to the time of Christ. In one scene Fingin, the Healer, ministers to the sorely wounded warrior, Cethern, and says, "A vain, arrogant woman gave you that wound."

> "I believe you are right," replies Cethern. "A tall, fair, long-faced woman with soft features came at me. She had a head of yellow

hair, and two gold birds on her shoulders. She wore a purple cloak folded about her, with five hands' breadth of gold on her back. She carried a light, stinging, sharp-edged lance in her hand, and she held an iron sword with a woman's grip over her head—a massive figure." (Quoted in Kinsella, 1970, p. 87)

It is true that this tableau leaves us with the image of a woman warrior, but we then have the opportunity of transforming that "massive" energy into a force that can support and cherish the other, both animate and inanimate. Our challenges are so formidable that a model painted in pastels will never be equal to them.

Nel Noddings (1995) expressed our goals so well when she wrote,

> Much of the school curriculum should be organized around themes of care: caring for self, caring for intimate others, caring for strangers and global others, caring for plants, animals, and the natural environment, caring for the human-made environment and caring for ideas. (p. 180)

This could serve as a fitting ending, but like life there is no conclusion. As long as there is human consciousness, there will always be crises and the search for adequate means to resolve them—and so we move on...

Discussion Suggestions

1. As you examine the projections of the U.S. Census Bureau, what impact do you think such a population shift will have on your personal life? On the society's economy? What challenges and opportunities do you see for the classroom teacher? How will the school curriculum differ from the present course of study?

2. Alfred North Whitehead wrote:

> When you are criticizing the philosophy of an epoch, do not chiefly direct your attention to those intellectual positions which its exponents feel it necessary explicitly to defend. There will be some fundamental assumptions which adherents of all the various systems within the epoch unconsciously presuppose. Such assumptions appear so obvious that people do not know what they are assuming because no other way of putting things has ever occurred to them.

Consider some of the assumptions under which at one time you were operating. If you have traveled, even in this country, you may have discovered that other groups of people did not share your convictions. What was your response? Were you uncomfortable? If this exposure did bring about changes in your thinking, how were you able to integrate this new perspective with valuable formerly acquired knowledge?

3. Are the interview and case study valid ways of obtaining scientific information? What strengths and weaknesses do they present when compared with other forms of data gathering?

4. Do you think that Educational Reconstruction has a "future?" Cognizant of the fact that many of its concepts run counter to present societal norms, could you imagine using the philosophy of Educational Reconstruction as a vehicle for your own thinking and acting?

5. What "myth" have you constructed for yourself as a mature adult? As an elderly person? Can you visualize yourself engaging in successful classroom teaching? Describe the picture in detail, including colors, sounds, and smells. What personal myth could move you in the direction of social-self-realization?

References

Belenky, M.F., B.M. Clinchy, N.R. Goldberger, & J.M. Tarule. (1986). *Women's Way of Knowing*. New York: Basic Books, Inc.

Brameld, T. (1947). "An Inductive Approach to Intercultural Values." *Journal of Educational Sociology*, Sept., 4-11.

Brameld, T. (1947). "Interculturral Democracy—Education's New Frontier." *The Educational Forum*, Nov., 67-73.

Brameld, T. (1950). *Patterns of Educational Philosophy*. Yonkers, NY: World Book.

Brameld, T. (1955). "Culture and Education." *The Journal of Higher Education*, Feb. 26, 59-68.

Brameld, T. (1972). "Education as Self-fulfilling Prophecy." *Phi Delta Kappan*, Sept., 8-11.

Brameld, T. (1974). *The Teacher as World Citizen*. Palm Springs, CA: E.T.C. Publications

Brameld, T. (1977). "Reconstructionism as Radical Philosophy of Education: A Reappraisal. *The Educational Forum*, Nov. 67-76.

Brameld, T. & M. Matsuyama. (1977). *Tourism as Cultural Learning: Two Controversial Case Studies in Educational Anthropology*. Washington, DC: University Press of America.

Conrad, D. (1994). "Educating with Community Murals." *Multicultural Education*, Fall, 7-39.

Daly, M. (1974). *Beyond God the Father*. Boston, MA: Beacon Press.

Day, J.C. (1991). "National Population Projections." *U.S. Census Bureau*. [Online]. Available: http:/www.census.gov/pub/population/pop-profile/natproj.html

Exter, T.G. (1993). "The Declining Majority." *American Demographics*, Jan., p. 59.

Glasersfeld, Ernst von. (1984). "An Introduction to Radical Constructivism." in P. Watzlawick (Ed.), *The Invented Reality*. New York: Norton.

Kinsella, T. (1970). *The Tain: Translated from the Irish Epic, Tain Bo Cuailnge*. Oxford, United Kingdom: Oxford Press.

Langsam, G.F. (1994). "The Community as Classroom: Personal Reflections of a Retired Reconstructionist Educator." *Teacher Education Quarterly*, Fall, 127-134.

Miller, J.B. (1976). *Toward a New Psychology of Women*. Boston, MA: Beacon Press.

Noddings, N. (1984). *Caring: A Feminine Approach to Ethics and Moral Education*. Berkeley, CA: University of California Press.

Noddings, N. (1993). *Educating for Intelligent Belief or Nonbelief*. New York: Teacher's College Press.

Noddings, N. (1995). *Philosophy of Education*. Boulder, CO: Westview Press.

Oakley, M.E. (1972). *Elizabeth Cady Stanton*. Brooklyn, NY: Feminist Press.

Postman, N. (1995). *The End of Education*. New York: Alfred A. Knopf.

Watzlawick, P. (1976). *How Real Is Real*. New York: Vintage Books.

CONTRIBUTING AUTHORS

Darrol Bussler is a professor of educational foundations at Mankato State University, Mankato, Minnesota. His research interests are integration of democratic practice in organizations, involvement of youth on policymaking boards and councils, and restorative justice. He currently serves as chairperson of The Society for Educational Reconstruction.

Frances L. O'Neil is a professor of psychology at Tunxis Community-Technical College, Farmington, Connecticut. She has long been involved in international education, with particular emphasis on the psychologies of East Asia. She is also in private practice as a counseling psychologist and is in the process of co-editing a book on problem-solving strategies. Active for many years in The Society for Educational Reconstruction, she currently is a member of the Society's Executive Committee.

Angela Raffel, author and lecturer on educational issues, is a professor in the Department of Education at the University of Bridgeport, Bridgeport, Connecticut, where she teaches philosophy of education, adolescent literature, and developmental reading. Her recent publications include "The Future of Charter Schools" and a monograph entitled *A Curriculum for the Twenty-First Century*. A former chairperson of The Society for Educational Reconstruction, she presently serves as the Society's recording secretary and on its archives committee.

Frank Andrews Stone is professor emeritus of international education at the University of Connecticut, Storrs, Connecticut, and a visiting professor at Trinity College, Hartford, Connecticut. He was a teacher and administrator at the American School for Turkish Youth, Tarsus, Turkey, from 1953 to 1966, and a visiting professor at Hacettepe University, Ankara, Turkey, during the 1969-1970 academic year. He has written twenty-two books and monographs and more than sixty articles and reports. He served as editor of *Cutting Edge*, the journal of The Society for Educational Reconstruction, for four years. He is a past chairperson of the Society, is currently a member of its Executive Committee, and in 1994 received the Society's Gertrude Langsam Award.

T. Mathai Thomas, a professor at the University of Bridgeport, Bridgeport, Connecticut, teaches courses in philosophy of education, community analysis, comparative education, and peace studies. He is author or co-author of six books, including *Images of Man: A Philosophic and Scientific Inquiry*. He was the first Secretary-Treasurer of The Society for Educational Reconstruction from 1969 to 1973 and has remained active in the organization ever since, currently serving on its Executive Committee.

ABOUT
THE SOCIETY
FOR EDUCATIONAL
RECONSTRUCTION

The Society for Educational Reconstruction (SER) is a voluntary non-political organization for encouraging personal, group, and social transformation through innovative and change-oriented education. It was founded in 1969. Its membership consists of concerned citizens and educators in many parts of the United States and elsewhere in the world, all committed to the purposes of SER and wishing to participate in activities designed to advance those purposes. Four central concepts shape the goals of SER:

1. Cooperative Power. SER is a support network for educators and citizens who function as social change activists. It encourages them to collaborate in order to assure that knowledge is being applied for moral purposes. It also seeks to aid them in overcoming the evil effects of agism, racism, sexism, and other types of unfair discrminiation in schools and society. SER members are involved in shared planning in order to achieve a better future for all humanity.

2. Global Order. Learning processes that respect human dignity and diversity are advocated by SER. Its members seek ways to end exploitation, violence, and nuclear proliferation in order to eradicate the chief causes of war by establishing social justice and world law. SER defends the rights of all to dissent and be different. It helps its members to transcend the limitations of narrow ideological and national allegiances in order to form a more global outlook encompassing all of humankind.

3. Self-transformation. Members of SER design and offer instruction

135

that enhances the creative potential of both learners and teachers. They stress developing the skills needed for effective intercultural communication, conflict resolution, and mutual understanding. They work to reconstruct existing institutions so that those institutions will become more convivial and inclusive. They advocate learning experiences that promote holistic social selfhood.

4. Social Democracy. It is the contention of SER that educational and social decisions should be democratically made. Its members labor to achieve equal access to educational and employment opportunities for all. They urge corporations and government agencies to increase their socially beneficial activities and cease their harmful operations. They strive for a fairer distribution of the world's resources and wealth, as well as for ecologically-sound policies.

— —

SER Membership Form

Name _____

Profession _____

Address _____

_____
(include Zip-code)

Type of Membership (please check your choice):
❏ Regular ($25 per year)
❏ Family ($35 per year)
❏ Full-time Student ($15 per year)
❏ Institution ($50 per year)

Please make checks for the amount indicated above payable to "The Society for Educational Reconstruction" and mail with this form to:

The Society for Educational Reconstruction
c/o Gaddo Gap Press
3145 Geary Boulevard, Suite 275
San Francisco, California 94118, U.S.A.